MEMOIRS
OF A
NOBODY

Nitram Drib

Editing, design, typesetting and publishing by UK Book Publishing

www.ukbookpublishing.com

ISBN: 978-1-916572-29-4

MEMOIRS
OF A
NOBODY

CONTENTS

For Emily and Lauren

INTRODUCTION

My earliest memories are climbing through the back doors of a dark green Commer Cob van with my siblings along with other children from our street. This was my dad's work van, and it was the weekend. He had carefully removed the company's water softener logos from the side of the vehicle to avoid being seen driving it privately, as he often took us kids, plus any other hangers-on from the road, and whisked us all off to the beach for the day.

How do I know I was only three years old? Because on 27th September 1962 a devastating event happened which would change our family perspective for ever. Aged just 35 years old, my dad died.

MY FAMILY HISTORY

My mother was born Pauline Bone on 18th April 1929. She was born in the front bedroom of 7 Fairthorn Terrace, which was later renamed 21 Wrecclesham Road, Farnham. She was tenth born from a family of 12 children, with four brothers and seven sisters, all of whom were born at home accompanied by a midwife. There were three bedrooms in the house, one for her parents, one with a double bed for three to sleep in, and one with a bunk bed for a further two, while downstairs were 'put you up' beds for three to sleep on. The eldest two, Bob and Reg, were often away in the army and on occasions some of her sisters who were in service in local houses, would sleep at their place of work. Her father Robert had two allotments, one opposite the house for growing vegetables and a second one down the back lane by some houses called The Hatches. On this one he kept chickens and rabbits, which provided a source of meat throughout the year. At the end of the terrace was a shop.

Mealtimes were a busy affair, with one table set in the kitchen and one table in the front room. To fit everyone in, a plank was laid across two chairs to provide extra seating. Mum's mother Alice was forever making meals and cooking. At Christmas Robert would have a barrel of beer in the front room which the postman was very fond of when he came by delivering their letters!

One evening there was a local fair in town at Castle Street, so Mum decided to go with Eileen Gardner, a schoolfriend. When she walked home, she was followed by a handsome young man called Victor, who slowly caught her up by the time she had reached the cemetery. He had spied her at the fair and decided he wanted to introduce himself to her and get to know her better. They walked on towards Wrecclesham Road and stopped at the Cox bridge which crossed the river Wey. This was a double bridge which had one arch spanning the river and one arch to allow the cows to move beneath the road. It was at this point that mum's father Robert came across the fields walking his two dogs, to which he shouted out "isn't it about bloody time you were in". Mum felt embarrassed and thought she wouldn't see Victor again as they had arranged to meet the following evening. However, Victor was at the meeting point, and they went to the County cinema to watch one film and then onto the Regal cinema to see another one.

Things progressed well and at the age of 21 Mum married Victor on 24th February 1951 at Wrecclesham church. Their first accommodation was a flat in Fishers Camp, Holybourne, which until 1947 had been a prisoner of war camp for German detainees housed in Nissen huts. The camp was empty by February 1948 and it was suggested that the structures already in place could be refurbished into local accommodation. Eventually, the Nissen huts were adapted, and families moved in. Fishers House was turned into flats while the Nissen huts were converted into basic living accommodation. It was a flat in Fishers House that Mum and Dad moved into. Inside the back door on the right was the kitchen with a door to a shared bathroom, which was unusable, and on the left was the sitting room while further up the passageway was a swing door onwards to the bedroom. Dad worked for the council as a plumber and in the evenings his second job was to go around the gas street lamps to turn them on in the evening and off in the morning.

Dad's parents were Jim and Rose, and Dad had a brother Dennis and sisters Pat and Margaret. Margaret married Mum's brother Leslie. My brother Brian was born in 1951 and my sister Angela followed in 1954; both lived at Fishers Camp until later that year when they all moved to Beechwood Road, a council house new build at the other end of Alton.

EARLY CHILDHOOD

I was born in January 1959. Two years before me in 1957, my brother Ian was born in the same month. Just over two years later my sister Julie arrived in the May.

My earliest memories, as mentioned, would have been from the summer of 1962 where just months later on 27th September Dad died unexpectedly. He had been at work when he felt unwell, and was brought home by a passing stranger, where he went to bed to lie down. He didn't recover and his death certificate stated coronary thrombosis, a blocking of the arteries which causes a heart attack.

The day my father was brought home from work, my sister Angela went in to kiss him goodnight and Brian went in and read to him a little. When Angela awoke in the morning and left her bedroom, Auntie Margaret, Dad's sister, was standing on the landing and broke the news that her dad had died. She went downstairs and Mum, sat on a wooden chair in the middle of the room, surrounded by her siblings, told her to go upstairs and get ready for school. That morning Brian, Angela and Ian all walked to school, Brian to Amery Hill, Ian was taken to Normandy Street School by Angela who then walked on to Alton County Junior School. Once in class, Angela was asked to take the register to the headmistress, and whilst out of the room, her classmates were told to 'be nice to Angela as her dad had just died'. When she returned her classmates commented that 'they were sorry to hear about her dad'. Angela never really understood the implications of someone dying, as this was all new to her. No one had sat her down and talked to her about death before.

Some days later Brian, Angela and Ian walked to school, and on returning home that day, when they entered, they were met by a house full of aunties and uncles. It had been the day of Dad's funeral and none of them were aware of it! I don't know whether it was the 'done thing' in those days that kids didn't attend funerals, or that Mum was advised badly, by her brothers and sisters, but ultimately, that decision would be resented by my older siblings for many years to come.

Life in Beechwood Road was never going to be the same again. Mum had a big decision to make – how was she going to manage as a single parent with five children?

Our house was a three-bedroomed semi-detached dwelling with a small front garden and a larger back garden which allowed plenty of room for a lawn area and space to grow a few vegetables. We had a swing on a patio area that ran along the length of the back of the house. We used to have jumping competitions off the swing which my brother Ian took to another level by bypassing the patio and landing on the rockery!

Inside the house, the front door led into the hallway, off of which was a bathroom. The lounge was on the right and the kitchen forwards through a passage. The sink was under the window overlooking the garden with the cooker to the left, and a larder opposite, sandwiching the back door. Outside, a shed and coal shed separated us from the neighbours' garden. Upstairs were three bedrooms and a toilet, with a loft hatch over the top of the stairs. Although modern by 1950s' standards, the windows were a single pane of glass in a metal frame, which glazed with ice on the inside on the coldest winter's nights. My bed would be covered with a sheet, then overlaid with woolly blankets, and an eiderdown to keep you warm. When my mum tucked me in so tight, I stayed in the same position until I woke up the next morning, unable to turn over! One night my sister Angela came into my room to say goodnight and tuck me in, and as I lay there, she told me to cover my ears over in case someone came along in the night and cut them off! Amusingly, I have never forgiven her for telling me that story as I still cover them now and I'm 64 years old! The glass in the windows was not the safety glass that you get nowadays. On one occasion my sister Julie was hanging out of the top front window at the top of the stairs when a gust of wind swung the window backwards, closing on her, her head smashed through the glass, framing her like a Rembrandt masterpiece! Luckily, apart from a few small cuts, she was not injured.

Times were hard in those early days, money was scarce, but Mum came through on every occasion, even managing to buy me a Johnny Seven gun when I was seven years old and paying our neighbours £5 for a new windscreen on their car when my brother Ian went to throw a stone, but it slipped from his hand backwards through their car windscreen. She made ends meet as best as she could, and often made items, like the stilts that we wanted, some wood, a few nails and a hammer and she had them made. To supplement the household income Mum found a part-time job cleaning offices early evenings at the Harp Lager brewery in town.

BOARDING SCHOOL

I was three years old when I was diagnosed with asthma. I recall having to take a small pill (which may have been Thanol, a muscle-relaxing pill) which was placed under my tongue and left to dissolve; however, it would take ages to do so and its taste was horrendous. It was very bitter and strong, which made taking it difficult. I would be doubled over struggling to breathe, gasping for breath, and my mother would be trying to get me to place it under my tongue.

"In a minute, in a minute," I would say. "Count to 10" – with which my mum would slowly count.

"1...2... 8...9...10," she would say. "Now open your mouth."

"Wait a moment, count again" and the whole process started again.

I don't know how many times we went through this scenario, but it must have been in the hundreds. Mum was a true saint for the patience she had with me.

My asthma didn't seem to be improving, so I regularly went to Alton General Hospital in Anstey Road, where I would be laid on a bed and my chest would be pummelled by a nurse, in a chopping motion or a clenched fist. They would repeat this on my back as well with the intention to loosen up the phlegm on my lungs.

One day Mum came home and sat me down. She told me that there were two schools which I could attend which would make my asthma better, one was in Scotland and the other was on the Isle of Wight. I wasn't being told that I had to go, but that the decision was mine alone. "Will it make me better?" I said. "Yes, the sea air will be good for you," replied Mum, and on that basis, I said yes, but chose the Isle of Wight option as this was much nearer to home.

After attending Alton County Junior school for the start of the new school term, in the November of 1968, at the age of nine years old, I set off for the first time to school in Ventnor with Mum and my sister Angela. We took the train to Portsmouth Harbour, where we embarked onto the ferry across to Ryde. From there we took the train to Shanklin. The trains were the old London underground carriages, and as we sped along the tracks, we felt like we were on trampolines, bouncing up and down uncontrollably, tears streaming down our faces from laughing our heads off! We then took the double decker bus onwards to Ventnor. Ventnor was established in the Victorian era set on the south side of St Boniface Down and built on steep slopes leading down to the sea.

My school was called St Catherine's in Grove Road, a residential Church of England school for 'delicate children', run by an Anglican community of Sisters. The school had a qualified headmaster and staff, seven classrooms, a library, dining room and kitchens, ample hardcourt play areas outside, along with two separate buildings, St Josephs and Elm Grove houses. Elm Grove sat at the top of the grounds high up, looking down onto the large grassy area stretching out before it. We had several indoor games such as billiards, draughts, chess, and card games. Football, cricket, and rounders were also played through the year.

That first night I settled into bed in a small room by the office of the duty nurse, crying myself to sleep. On every subsequent future return, those first few nights were very difficult, me as a nine-year-old boy, attending boarding school in a strange place away from my family, I cried myself to sleep regularly. I couldn't imagine placing my children of that age into a similar situation – my heart would be tearing itself apart with anguish! Each dormitory had between eight and ten beds in, which I settled into quietly, and being a shy boy, I tended to watch what happened rather than getting involved with any mischief. One night, one of the boys announced that he was going to glue up his foreskin to see what would happen. We thought no more of it until later that night he awoke in pain needing the toilet but was unable to go! One of the nurses had to assist him, a prank I'm sure he never repeated.

The bathroom was located above the kitchens and had three baths in, and on bath night we were usually assisted by carers who would ensure we either bathed or had our hair washed. On one such occasion we were left to our own devices, I was in one bath and Christopher was in another. He decided to slide forwards and backwards which sent the water sploshing over the edge of the bath. I did the same but stopped soon after, while he found much amusement continuing in his endeavours. Unfortunately, we didn't consider the consequences of our actions until we were marched downstairs into the kitchen to be shown the water streaming down from the ceiling light fittings! We were punished but I cannot remember how.

At nine years old, I weighed 3st 8lbs and stood 4ft 3ins tall. I liked to play football and played in the school team. In the team with me were Ian Major, Christopher Levick, Stephen Gilmartin, Mark Pearce, Barrington Burrell, Kevin Simpson, Wayne Fletcher, Craig Hyden, Timmy O'Brien, and Kevin Cannon. We played in an Isle of Wight schools cup competition and got to the final, which was played on a scaled-down pitch in Newport, where we lost 1-0.

One of the boys' uncles was the great Peter Osgood who played for Chelsea at the time; we were very excited when he once came to visit.

Those pupils who were well behaved, which included me (despite the bathroom incident), were once treated to a day visit to Southampton Football club at The Dell, where we had a tour of the ground. I was mesmerized by the story of the underground river running beneath the pitch from goalmouth to goalmouth, which flooded during the war when a bomb landed on the pitch. It was due to this visit that I became a Southampton fan, and although there have been some good times over the years, currently it's pretty depressing following them. Before this visit, I had an affinity with West Ham, purely because I was told by my friends that I looked like Martin Peters, so on that basis, my first football shirt was a West Ham one. I am aware that changing support to a different team is not normal practice, but apart from a passing resemblance to a World Cup Final scorer, there was no other connection.

One memory I have is of Barrington, having done something wrong, was chased by the housemaster through the day room, and approaching the small window-panelled patio doors, stretched his arms out to push them open. However, the doors remained steadfast, and his hands smashed through the glass, cutting his wrists badly. There were numerous other incidents that occurred during my time at the school. Once a large group of pupils went into town one Saturday and decided to shoplift anything they could, bringing their ill-gotten gains back to the school. They were reported and as a result, the goods were returned to the shops and the town was off-limits to pupils for some time.

My mother would come over to the island and visit at weekends during the term, bringing Julie, Ian and Angela on various occasions, and would stay at a house further up Grove Road on the right-hand side. This was owned by a Mrs Whittington, who put up visiting families on the recommendation of the school. On these occasions we would spend time visiting all the local places of interest; this included Blackgang Chine which claims to be the oldest amusement park in the UK. Opened in 1843, the park was built on unstable terrain and the cliffs are currently eroding at a rate of 3.5 metres per year. On subsequent visits to the park some years later, it was evident that previous attractions had been moved inland and fenced off pathways led to the cliff edge. The Needles and its lighthouse were a spectacular sight, and Alum Bay nearby, was famous for its coloured sands. You could buy a small glass lighthouse and fill it with layered coloured sands, all kept in place by a small cork. Godshill Model Village was fantastic, intricate model houses depicting the Godshill and Shanklin villages. As a young lad Carisbrooke Castle stirred the imagination, and my love of historical buildings still lives on today through my English Heritage membership. Brading Wax Works Museum was a very dark and scary place – I remember a coffin with a hand poking out of it and a skeleton playing the organ. We also visited

Sandown beach and had walks on St Boniface Downs, the highest point on the island. On one occasion Mum and I had taken a double decker bus on the island, only to find that when we had alighted, I had left our camera on the seat. With haste, we quickly grabbed the nearest taxi and sped off trying to catch the bus up, which we eventually did, and retrieved the camera.

There were two major global events that I recall while staying at St Catherine's. The first was on 20th July 1969, where we were all taken up to the big house at the top of the school grounds, called Elm Grove. We were placed in front of a television to watch the historical moon landing, at 8.17pm. The second occasion was the 1970 World Cup competition held in Mexico in June of that year, where I recall seeing the England v West Germany match where England held a 2-0 lead only to lose 3-2; my first real disappointment from a football match. I was, after all, a new supporter of Southampton following my visit to The Dell previously, so the first of many let-downs. I don't remember the 1966 World Cup – I was recovering from having my appendix taken out in April of that year, and we didn't rent a television until after the event.

I spent a total of two years at St Catherine's, and each term I had a school report on my progress. I excelled in English, Science and Nature, and Handwork (two wicker trays made by me over 50 years ago and still being used are testament to that fact!).

Although those two years were hard on my soul and mind, I feel that it gave me a strength to draw upon in later life, to be comfortable with my own self, and helped to develop me into who I am today. I'd learnt at St Catherine's the art of negotiation when mixing with my peers, and this would develop into my working life.

CHILDHOOD
ENTERTAINMENT

Fun times in my early teen life were of playing games with my siblings. Brian and Angela were much older than myself, so I had more interaction with Ian which involved the game of Subbuteo Football. To give a more realistic playing pitch, Ian and I went to town and returned with a large-sized sheet of hardboard which we glued the Subbuteo pitch to. We had progressed from the cloth pitch laid on a carpet or table – you couldn't have George Best or Mick Channon readying to shoot and being tripped up by a two-foot tidal wave of carpet hidden beneath the pitch! We set up a fixture list mirroring the old Division 1, playing each game, and recording the results, producing a league table just like the real one. Inevitably, we never fully completed it, so neither my Southampton nor Ian's Manchester United won the league title. I would also paint the Subbuteo players so that they had different kits – it saved buying more teams. I went on to buy the Subbuteo Table Rugby edition and the Cricket Test Match Edition, but only ever attempted to play these by myself. The Rugby game remains pretty much untouched in the loft to this day, but the Cricket game took on a whole new life of itself. Not being satisfied with the scoreboard provided in the game which had circular counters for runs scored, wickets fallen, and overs bowled, I concocted a scoreboard which I stuck over the plastic front that had additional slots for batsmen's scores, overs bowled, last wicket score, how out, and last batsman's score. Then, playing on my own, I would place the ball on the small wire triangle behind the bowler's figure, hold the bat with one hand and flick the bowler forward with my other hand propelling the ball toward the wicket. Simultaneously, I would swing the bat hoping to hit the ball, then record the outcome, either as runs, no score, leg bye, bowled or caught by a fielder. Each ball bowled was then written on a score chart as per a proper scorer at a cricket match, runs, dot ball etc. Then I would change the numbers on the scoreboard with carefully cut-to-size pieces of paper, which I would insert into the slots I had created, to reflect the score.

Another game I used to make up by myself involved bubble-gum cards. I suppose I became interested in collecting cards after my mum used to give me the cards inside Brooke Bond Tea packets. I have many tea card books from many subjects that were promotional tools used to get consumers to buy Brooke Bond tea. This transgressed into me buying packets of bubble-gum which had cards in, produced either by Anglo Confectionery or A & BC, covering subjects such as Batman, Tarzan, Captain Scarlett, The Horse, Space, Battle cards and Football cards. I would lay out a horse racing track using these cards in a circular pattern, then carefully cut out a horse shape from a piece of paper doubled over – this enabled the horse to stand up. After numbering the horses, I would throw a dice and each one took turns to move, the number of moves corresponding with the cards laid out along the side of the track. Each horse had different odds and would fall in the race if they landed on a fence, denoted by a row of cards across the track. This was all done for my own amusement, probably dreamt up after watching the Grand National, as I never benefited financially! I certainly had a lot of patience – after buying plenty of Airfix 00 scale soldier armies, I would painstakingly paint them one by one in their colours.

Most games I played involved my sister Julie. She had a small till given to her as a present, with make-believe money in. We used to empty Mum's larder of tins and packets and play shops, me entering the 'shop' and Julie serving me. We also played Monopoly regularly, but having never read the rules properly, any fines were not paid into the bank, but put on the free parking space, whereupon, if you landed on that square you took all the money on it. I'm sure many other players did something similar; I mean, who reads the rules anyway! If I was winning the game, I used to give Julie a £1 note and say, "here you are, go and get yourself some fish and chips"!

My most used toy was Action Man; I had bought lots of different costumes over time – the deep-sea diver, paratrooper, sailor, and combat soldier. I regularly kitted him out in his parachute costume, and from a top window, would send him hurtling to his death as the parachute failed to open in time! Julie's favourite was a Sindy doll, and like me, would imagine a world where Sindy lived, sometimes in unison with Action Man. Julie would set up her Sindy with all the accompaniments of her doll's house, and, when she had left the room, my Action Man would enter the living room and destroy all her belongings, scattering them across the room, throwing hand grenades and shooting Sindy dead! Then he would exit as quickly as he had arrived before Julie returned and seeing the carnage would run to Mum crying! Although this might have seemed a bit harsh, we played well together, and formed a strong bond which is still present today.

Not everything was so pleasant. On one occasion, Ian had annoyed me, so, grabbing a fountain pen, I chased him up the stairs, flicking the pen in his direction, but never really hitting him. When Mum came home, she noticed spots of ink all up the landing wallpaper, and not having the money to redo the whole wall, she painstakingly cut each spot of ink out and stuck a square back into its place. Because I was a sickly child, I managed to get away with my actions more so than my siblings; this was not something I expected, and I would have been happy to take my punishment just the same as anyone else, but Mum had a soft spot for me due to my health, a fact that didn't go unnoticed by my brothers and sisters!

SCHOOL

My first school was Normandy Street Infant school, now called Alton Infant School. I have vivid memories of receiving the slipper for disobedience. It started in the playground where there were climbing bars in a dome shape, which we were told to keep off. My friend Richard decided to hang from them, which I copied, and being caught we were marched to the headmaster's office where we had the slipper smacked across our legs. A couple of years later in the playground, Richard gave me a birthday card, and upon opening it a thruppenny bit emerged. I immediately said, "Is that all?", before correcting myself for being ungrateful. I was mortified with myself for making such a remark, and to this day, I hate receiving presents, I prefer to give a present than receive one. I haven't celebrated my birthday for years, with it being in early January. I would rather gloss over it and hope that no-one turns up to give me presents or spend money on me.

After Normandy Street school I attended Alton County Junior school from the ages of seven to nine until I went off to the Isle of Wight. One defining memory of attending this school was myself, my sister Julie and a boy called Andrew. After leaving school we had walked with Andrew down Littlefield Road and turned right onto Anstey Road. We were all due to catch the bus. Julie and I would normally get off at the Butts while Andrew would continue on to Four Marks. As we approached the bus stop, which was on the opposite side of the road outside the Alton House Hotel, the double decker bus pulled up. Without hesitation or warning, when we were opposite the junction with Paper Mill Lane, Andrew immediately panicked and ran across the road without looking, only to be hit full on by an ambulance which went over the top of him. We just didn't know what to do, as the ambulance crew set to work on him. Ironically we caught that same bus home and only later discovered that he had died. There was no trauma counselling in those days for us, we had to work through our feelings on our own. At the coroner's inquest, the coroner commented in his summing up to the jury: "He may have seen the bus coming and suddenly dashed across the road to catch it. Children of eight sometimes do this sort of thing, as they can think of only one thing at the time. He was oblivious of the dangers". Only I knew why he made that fatal dash across the road. He had already told me that his mum was going to be on the bus, and presumably thinking he might miss it, ran into the road. As a result of this tragic accident, it shaped how in later life when I had my own children, I drilled road safety into them whenever we crossed a road.

When I returned from St Catherine's, I went straight into secondary school, Amery Hill, at 11 years of age. I never really enjoyed school, any school, it was just an inconvenience in the day to have to present myself at this day release prison, or that's what it felt like. I was a shy person, never really making my views known, but I didn't want to be the subject of a bully either. I recall a rare occasion when I had to visit the toilet while in class time. I left Mr Walker's history class and made my way to the loos. Once inside I encountered the school bully Freddie. Freddie was the archetypal bully, small in stature, looking to fight anyone anytime. "Come on, Martin, give me a fight to see if you can beat me," he said. I had never had a fist fight in my life and wasn't about to start. "That's ok, Freddie," I said, "you will beat me easily, you're far better than me" was my reply, and with that I made a hasty retreat. A little bit of flattery did no harm, and if I'm honest, a lot of truth in my response and an element of negotiation starting to emerge. I was in the third class of the top tier, classes were graded ROY, GBI, VS, initials of the colours of the rainbow, although I'm sure the S at the end stood for Stupid! I was in class Y, not the top but far from the worst. I believe it was in this class that I came to realise that making witty remarks kept you in good keeping with the tougher kids, so my witticism started to take shape. Any opportunity to make a joke out of a situation and make others laugh increased my confidence and put me in that bracket of 'Birdy? Oh, he's alright'. I believe that I was never picked on at school because of my joking, and as I got older joking about and having a laugh became the norm.

TEENAGE YEARS

Outside of school, I started attending Chawton Youth Club, set up to give teenagers some focus on activities that didn't involve criminal acts. Ultimately, the pure existence of the youth club resulted in just such a thing. They ran a tuck shop in the club, which was situated in the village hall, and when it wasn't in operation the sweets were kept on a top shelf in a tall, locked metal cupboard. I will start by stating that I was never the instigator of such events, but I did partake in them; I was easily led. We discovered that with some force applied to the top of the metal door by pulling it outwards, we could get our hands inside and snatch as much of the sweets as we could, Curlywurlys, Cadbury's Fudge etc. This worked well on several occasions until, due to the regular force applied, the doors started to bow outwards, never meeting in the middle. Once the leader had discovered this theft, we denied it all, and the confectionery was removed from our reach. This also reminds me of the small shop that used to exist at the end of Tanhouse Lane and Amery Hill. We all used to pile into the shop after school and someone would ask the elderly lady owner for an ice lolly which was in a freezer in the rear of the shop. While she was retrieving the ice lolly, we would stuff our bags full of sweets from the counter, and upon her return, behave as if nothing had happened. I recall arriving home with a duffle bag full of various goodies, an action that even today I feel remorse for, the guilt and shame for my involvement in theft from a helpless elderly lady who was just trying to make a living running a shop. Again, I was easily led, but that is a poor excuse, and I have immense respect for the elderly today.

At the youth club I had access to a table tennis table and started to play regularly, becoming quite good at it. As a result, I started playing for Chawton Youth Club B team in the Alton league which had five divisions. In my very first game, in a farcical situation, and with tears streaming down my face from laughing so much, I won 21-0, 21-0. If this was the standard I would be facing, this game is easy! We reached the Junior Final that season 73/74 where myself, David and Les lost to Odiham Youth club 6-3, with me finishing unbeaten and scoring our three points. In the 1974/5 season I had moved up to the A side, and after playing 20 games I had personally scored 52 points out of 60, the team finished 5th in the league and reached the final of the Under 21 cup where we lost to Treloar's 3-6. My stock had risen and in the 1975/6 season I began playing for Treloar's E team in division 2, along with Bruce who lived around the corner from me. That season we finished mid-league but we did reach the Losers Plate final playing Nalgo C and finally experiencing a cup final victory with a 5-4 win; we also won the Under 21 cup 5-4 v Stroud. In the 1976/7 season in division 2 we finished 3rd in the league, and on a personal note I scored 45 points from a possible 54 and notably made the headlines in the Alton Herald with a 'Bird on Song' headline denoting my success in one particular league game. We also reached the Under 21 cup final again, losing to Stroud Youth 3-6. The 1977/8 season was my last one, table tennis was interfering in my involvement with girls, and although I had a good season on a personal level, our team failed to win anything.

I also played football for Chawton Youth Club in a local league; however, we were dreadful. Our first game of the season was an 18-0 loss, and during the course of the whole season we had 0 wins and 0 draws, recording further losses of 22-0 and 36-0, with our best result being a 3-4 loss. During these games I would often slice the ball into my own net on purpose, just to feel more involved – no one on my team suspecting that I did it on purpose. They just thought that I was a rubbish footballer!

Around this time, I had taken up working on a Sunday morning doing a paper-round, not just the local estate delivering papers, but the village of Selborne, which required cycling from home to the village along the B3006 a total of four miles, leaving at 7am. The thought of making that journey some 47 years later along that narrow road, and with the speed of the traffic today, would terrify me now. In those days traffic was considerably lighter early in the morning; however, the journey was made harder because I was riding a tradesman's bike. For anyone not familiar with one, at the front of the handlebars was a square metal basket with a wooden base that my papers would sit on, coupled with the fact that there were no gears on the bike, it was just pure pedal power that propelled you up the hills. At least I didn't have to cycle with a basket full of papers; these were delivered by car in advance, the first bundle was dropped at Goslings Croft, the first estate on entering the village, and the second bundle at the White House shop, a Grade 2 listed building further on through the village (not to be confused with Gilbert White's Museum). The papers were already numbered and put in order of delivery by the paper shop in Alton. On delivering them I would collect the money, or mark in my book if they didn't pay, and the total was carried over to the next week. If their debt accumulated too much, then I would need to knock on the door to get payment. When I had cycled through the village and delivered them all, I then had to cycle back to Alton to the far end of town to the paper shop to total up my money. By the time I had got home I had cycled at least

10 miles and would then spend an hour lying on the settee snoozing while Mum would Hoover up the living room around me. Even now, when I hear a hair dryer or a Hoover, I have the urge to lie down and cover my ears up and snuggle down in the warmth of a blanket. On the occasional Sunday I might not be feeling well, and Julie would then do the papers for me, she would have been only 14 at her youngest, quite an achievement for her. There were also times when she would accompany me (I had to pay her from my wages) but it meant we could finish quicker. There was one house, just past Goslings Croft, up some steps to a row of bungalows, where the guy would come to the door wearing an open dressing gown and a vest, but no underwear, and yes, I was cruel enough to send her to the door every time! At home we had some fun with the bike and Julie would sit in the basket while I cycled around. However, one day the handlebar snapped so my seat swung left while Julie and the handlebars swung right, riding along like a clown at the circus on his trick bike! Needless to say, the shop never got to hear how it happened!

Myself and my friend David also started working at Chawton House as gardeners. Chawton House was known as the great house in Jane Austen's letters, and she used to dine there with her brothers and sisters. Jane's brother Edward was adopted by Thomas and Catherine Knight who were childless and made Edward their heir. Jane Austen's house is also in the village just along the road. We were employed by Mrs Knight to keep the grounds tidy. One such job involved sitting on the petrol-driven lawnmower and whizzing around the vast grounds cutting the grass, a task we both enjoyed and shared between us. We were never asked to tend the herb garden at the back of the house, but I did cut the grass in the graveyard of Chawton Church, which also sits in the grounds. Jane's sister Cassandra and her mother are buried here, and at the back of the graves lay the pet cemetery with the graves of many dogs, the headstones scattered under the trees. On occasions I was sent to Jane Austen's house to tidy the garden. On hot days Mrs Knight used to invite us into the house, through the front door into a wood-panelled corridor, leather fire buckets hanging from hooks above, and into a kitchen area where she would make us a soda stream drink.

COLLEGE

I left school in the summer of 1975 with the grand total of one 'O' Level and four CSEs. The 'O' Level was in maths and was achieved by sitting next to Anthony, the brainiest boy in the class; this was like having a personal tutor mentoring you. He certainly helped to drag me through the course. But my achievements were nothing to be proud of, I certainly wasn't going to be a brain surgeon or nuclear physicist; but likewise, I had no idea of what I wanted to do. I had attended careers evenings at Amery Hill, where a standard list of employment positions were bandied about. Did I want to be a policeman? A fireman? A dustman? I didn't bloody know, what do you think, sir! Armed with an empty head I was well qualified to do nothing at all, so with that I enrolled to attend Queen Mary's College in Basingstoke – at least this would delay having to decide for another two years. Due to Mum's financial position, I also qualified for a grant which helped with, wait, what did it help with? I really don't remember, but it was certainly welcome as far as Mum was concerned.

So, in September 1975 I attended college. Everyone attending from Alton caught a double decker bus the 15 miles to Basingstoke every day. That first year I studied Economics and English Language 'O' Level and Pure Mathematics with Statistics 'A' Level. Along with this we were given a timetable which included a few 'non' subjects and some free period time. The 'A' Level maths was a two-year course, and by chance I befriended and sat next to a guy called Graeme, who, you guessed it, was the brainiest lad in the class! That first year we used to play cards every lunchtime, numbers-based games kept the mind sharp. That first year I obtained passes in both the 'O' Levels I sat.

My first, what I would call 'real girlfriend' was Caron, who ran around with Amanda and Sara. All three were Alton Convent Girls school attendees – just the thought of a convent girl brought the testosterone levels up a notch. My friend Graham was seeing Sara, and although I don't remember my first meeting with Caron, it probably came about as a result of hanging around as a group. Caron was a beautiful girl and a good kisser, not that I had any experience at kissing. She was of Far eastern appearance and had a lovely skin shade and complexion. She lived in New Barn Lane, an unadopted road in one of the most exclusive areas of town, and her father worked at the stock exchange in London. She was far too good for me, and I struggled to hang onto her after just a few weeks. In the summer of

1976, we decided to go to a horse show jumping event at Rotherfield Park at East Tisted. While lying about on the grass watching the events, my friend Paul came to join us, and the two of them didn't stop talking. The flirting was deafening, the sexual chemistry was oozing, and I lay there watching this union take place, unable to intervene. Of course, inside I was feeling incredibly jealous, wishing I could be left alone with her. I was left alone eventually, as a single guy! Paul and Caron began a tempestuous relationship over the next few years. They were made for each other, perfectly suited, but also perfectly toxic, breaking up and reuniting on numerous occasions over the following years.

Soon after, my friend Graham and Sara parted ways, and although unplanned, I started dating Sara. She was a year younger than me so still had to finish her schooling. She lived in Linnets Way, opposite Amery Hill school playing fields, with her mum Peggy. Peggy was widowed, her husband had died sometime before. Peggy and her husband had had another daughter born before Sara; however, she had died young from leukaemia, so by the time Sara was born her mum was 40 years old. They had been publicans running the Crooked Billet at Hook and then The Crown pub at Odiham, which has now been converted into private housing. Peggy had a gentleman caller called Mike, who drove a Nissan Sunny. Sara referred to him as 'uncle'; however, there wasn't any family connection, and we used to speculate if there was any romance between them. We quickly became an item, seeing each other regularly, and a highlight of the week would be going out to a country pub and having something 'in the basket'. The popular pub meals those days were either chicken, sausage, or scampi 'in the basket', a plastic wicker shaped basket filled with the food of your choice with chips. If we were going upmarket for a meal, we would put on our best clothes, me in my claret-coloured velvet jacket and tie, Sara in her best dress, and we would book a table at the Bush Hotel in Farnham, where we would have a prawn cocktail starter, a steak meal and black forest gateau for dessert. We also frequented Lakeside Country Club at Frimley Green, where, on more than one occasion we saw The Drifters perform their repertoire of songs, accompanied by a meal. I would be wearing my velvet jacket again, which was part of the dress code for entry, while the auditorium was predominantly a shade of red, with lights dimmed accordingly. Our relationship progressed, and we spent plenty of time together. In September 1976 Sara enrolled at St Mary's College as well, so we travelled together on the bus daily. I continued my 'A' Level maths course plus took English Literature 'O' Level and 'AO' History. Our relationship flourished into the following year, and although relatively new, was going nicely, until I became aware that she preferred to spend time during lunch with a lad called Guy. I felt tremendously jealous, my heart felt crushed, and my emotions went through the roof. I remember sitting on the bus next to her, returning from college discussing our relationship, totally and utterly unable to stop crying, oblivious to all around me. I had no idea who was aware of my plight, I was trying to make sense of it all. I was also quoting the words to love songs to highlight my feelings through all the tears, unable to fashion my own thoughts into anything sensible. I recited to Sara the words of the song 'A Thing Called Love' by Johnny Cash about a giant man brought to his knees by love. Of course, it bore no resemblance to myself at all, but I wanted to say, 'I love you'. I even had a double lesson in some nondescript subject one afternoon so it was agreed with the teacher that I could transfer from that lesson into a lesson that both Sara and Guy were attending so that I could keep an eye on proceedings. However, it didn't seem to work out well, so I advised the teacher that I would return to my original lesson, but didn't attend at all, giving me extra time off. At least something good came of my jealousy. Nothing came about from Sara's liaisons with Guy, but it did strengthen my feelings even more towards her. I had fallen in love. We finished the end of college term in June, and we spent the summer together.

On 17th August I had arranged to meet Sara at Alton train station in the morning for a day out in London; however, when she arrived I had to break the news to her that Elvis Presley had died. She was so upset, she didn't believe me and thought I was joking. That day in London in Carnaby Street I bought a Mexican jacket made famous from the TV programme Starsky and Hutch. We also called it a Starsky jacket, and I took pride in wearing it around town in Alton; I never saw anyone other than myself wearing one.

After leaving college my future was now rudderless and I had to decide where my life was going. Sara went back to college for her second year while I went about trying to secure a job. I still had no idea what I wanted to do, but having achieved a maths 'A' Level pass, I looked at trainee accountancy positions even though these required two 'A' Levels, and although I attended numerous interviews, I was never successful.

Around this time, Mum had been encouraged to attend ballroom dancing evenings, through her work at Harp Lager brewery. Some of her colleagues were already regulars, and two guys, Bill and Dick, were keen to take her along. She started going along with them both, and both of them had a romantic interest in Mum. They would dance her off her feet throughout the evening, but there was only ever going to be one winner, and that was Bill. Eventually Bill would call on his own and pick Mum up before going off for the evening. When they returned in Bill's Mini Clubman, Julie and I would race up the stairs to peer out through the window to see if they were kissing; we used to laugh at the thought of it happening. Bill turned out to be a wonderful, kind, and thoughtful person. He had volunteered for the RAF at age 17 before transferring to the army two years later where he served in Singapore, India, and Hong Kong. His Far Eastern tours involved guarding Japanese POWs and taking them from Stanley prison to dismantle the guns around the island. After the war, as a member of the British Royal Legion, he became standard bearer on Remembrance Sunday, a position that made him very proud. Apart from dancing, he loved playing golf and tending an allotment at Borovere Gardens near the Butts. Their relationship blossomed over time and on 5th September 1981 they got married. Many years later I used to joke to Mum that she didn't want Dick!

MY FIRST EMPLOYMENT

One day Mum came home and told me that there was a sign in the window of Key Markets supermarket looking for trainee managers. I secured an interview with the manager Mr B and, after being offered the job, I started in the branch in October with a view to working in the various departments, learning each trade as I went on to a possible management position. My first employment was in the grocery department where I worked under Ken, the grocery manager, and alongside Flave who worked on pricing the goods. There were no bar-codes in those days, so every item had to be priced individually. The stock was transferred from the loading bay in a lift to the warehouse where it was loaded onto a roller conveyor belt. Flave would wield her cutting knife on the boxes to open them up, then as quick as a flash price each item with the gun. Flave was a very open person, often detailing the dalliances she had with her husband while driving home late at night, stopping in a layby because she felt horny! Her method was to shock, something that I used myself on occasions when I grew older, although at 18 years old (and still a virgin) I more than likely blushed. I worked on the grocery department through into 1978, pricing up stock, shelf-filling, controlling stock and order, and building displays.

A few years previously, my auntie and uncle along with their two children had emigrated to South Africa and were flying into the UK for a holiday and to visit family. I had volunteered to drive up to Heathrow Airport with my mum (I had not long passed my driving test) while my Uncle Bob would also drive his car so we had enough room to transport them all back. It was to be on the Friday morning so I asked Ken if he would let Mr B know that I would be late into work because I was going to Heathrow. Friday morning arrived; I drove up to Heathrow Airport, picked up my relatives and drove them back to Alton. I managed to arrive at work about lunchtime and went to see Ken.

"Hi Ken, did you tell Mr B why I would be late in today?" I asked.

"No, I told him you were ill," he replied. "You better go and see him, he's on the shop floor now."

So off I trundle, down to the shop floor where I spy him checking the shelves.

"Mr B, I'm so sorry I'm late into work today, I've been sick all night long, but I know Fridays are our busiest day so as I felt slightly better, I've come in to help," I stated.

"Oh," he exclaimed, "I thought you had gone to Heathrow Airport to pick up your relatives!"

"No, I didn't go because I was ill," I replied, my face now going a deep shade of red, burning my skin so much I'm surprised he didn't get a suntan from the glow!

"Really, Ken said you were driving them back," he reiterated as he could see my discomfort.

Fuck! I'd passed the point of no return, got to keep going! "No, I've been sick all night."

He walked away; meanwhile I'm left hoping the floor would open up and swallow me whole to get me out of the most embarrassing moment of my life! (For now!)

After I'd served my time on the grocery department I moved onto the dairy section, responsible for cheeses, yoghurts etc. One day I went into the stock room for some additional supplies when out of the corner of my eye I noticed an egg box, sitting there with the lid of the box moving up and down on its own. Shocked, I moved closer to inspect it, carefully and slowly lifting up the lid to peep inside. To my horror, hundreds of maggots spilled out onto the floor. I reeled backwards, almost retching. I quickly disposed of the evidence in the bin – so much for stock rotation! After the dairy section I moved onto the frozen food section, responsible for planograms, stock levels and ordering. One of the benefits of running the department was that if any stock was damaged, I could take it home, along with any bread dated that day, which was offered to staff for free. At times the freezer in my mum's house couldn't fit another frozen pea or loaf of bread in! While running the department, sales reps from various companies like Birds Eye, Findus and Youngs would visit the store and I would place our order with them. Roy from Findus called one day and told me that they were looking for sales reps for the area and that I should apply for the position as I had good product knowledge already and this would be an advantage over other applicants.

On the 17th of September 1979 I started my career as a salesman for Findus, on the grand wage of £3,000, which by June 1980 had risen to £3,860. I was happy at Findus, the job came with a company car and the company ran a depot from Chandlers Ford, just 25 miles down the road. I used a pool car at first as I had to wait for my new car to be delivered, but once it was ready, a colleague, Tim, came with me to collect it. A brand-new light blue Vauxhall Chevette, which Tim insisted on driving back to the depot. Unfortunately, while driving down The Avenue into Southampton, Tim made an illegal right turn and hit an oncoming car, I hit my head on the front window frame – we didn't have to wear seatbelts in those days – and the car had to spend weeks being repaired. As punishment, Tim had to give me his car until it was repaired.

My role was to call on multiple grocers, regional grocers, and independents to obtain orders and then radio the order back to the depot for a 24-hour delivery service. In those days we called on Tesco stores directly and obtained orders in the branch. Our big launch that year was French Bread Pizza, which was a phenomenal success. The stock was flying out of the stores and Findus struggled to keep up with demand. Our marketing department also came up with another fabulous idea. In those days beef burgers consisted of 80% or less beef, the rest was made up of other meats and rusk, a yeast-less bread that is baked hard and used to bulk up the contents, reducing costs. In addition, there would be seasoning, and flavouring added. Our marketing department came up with the 'Findus 90% beef beefburger'. The meat content was 100% beef which was a higher beef content than any other burger on the market. The 90% referred to the percentage of the burger that was beef, the remaining 10% content contained seasoning, flavours, and content essential to making a burger stay in one piece. What Findus were trying to explain to the consumers was that this burger was pure beef which made up 90% of the total content. We had a big launch and were presented with a plaque containing a mounted knife and an inscription '90% BEEF BEEFBURGERS LAUNCH 1980'. This was going to be so great, the best burger in the UK, the burger to beat all others. All initially went well until later that year, Birds Eye brought out the same burger but called it Birds Eye 100% Beef Beefburger! Which burger would you buy if they were laid side by side? Our marketing department had tried to be too honest in their statement – it was 100% beef, but the beef only made up 90% proportion of the burger.

Inflation in 1980 was 18%, there was a recession on and on 24th November I was notified that I was being made redundant – 'last in, first out' they said. It was devastating news, and on visiting Sara later that day, Peggy's words were 'that bloody Margaret Thatcher!' However, Findus were more than good to me, my settlement included four weeks' notice pay, four weeks' statutory pay and nine weeks ex gratia pay all tax free, a total of 17 weeks which equated to nearly 6 months' take-home pay. I spent December at home making a dart board cupboard, went on a trip to Skipton in Yorkshire to a friend's wedding, and felt sad when John Lennon was murdered.

RELATIONSHIPS

My relationship with Sara had been going well. I used to spend all day Saturday at her house where we would make a Vesta Chop Suey or Chow Mein meal at lunchtime. Peggy would go to work on a Saturday at a small boutique clothes shop at the top of Crown Hill which enabled us to have some afternoon delight uninterrupted. This backfired on one occasion when Peggy, who had been feeling under the weather, came home early from work. We were lying naked on the living room floor when the doorbell went. Sara jumped up and looked through the net curtains. "It's Mum!" she yelped. Peggy, on getting no response, puts her key in the lock, we can hear it rattling. I jumped up and grabbed my clothes, Sara somehow managed to get her top and skirt on. Me naked, ran up the open plan stairs into the bathroom. Peggy entered the room through the small porch. I could hear them talking as I hid in the bathroom, where I decided to wait for the next five minutes, pretending to be busy. I got dressed then realised I had Sara's knickers with me. Putting them in my pocket I flushed the toilet and casually strolled downstairs. "Oh, hi, I thought I heard the door go," I said. I sat on the settee while Peggy sat perched on the arm of a chair. She had a look of thunder on her face as small talk was spoken. Did she see my white arse disappearing up the stairs? God, I hope not. Being 40 years older than Sara and having lost a young child, Peggy was protective towards her daughter, and she ruled her with a strong arm. Was I leading Sara astray? Heck no, we were young and in love, our hormones were taking over and exploring our bodies naturally led to sex although at this stage we were still virgins.

I was 19 when I lost my virginity to Sara, and she to me. I had been pestering her for full sex for some time, but she had been reluctant to do so. Contraception was an issue, she had no reason to be on the pill, so I took the decision out of her hands. I had been into some of the chemists in town to look at buying condoms; however, like any young man, being served by a female was an embarrassment. It reminded me of when I was 15 and I wanted to buy a pornographic magazine. I would enter the newsagent, scan the magazine rack, and make my decision which one to buy. Then I would pretend to be looking at other mags while keeping an eye on the till area. When there were no other customers about, I would quickly grab the chosen mag and rush to the till, pay for it, and not being challenged about my age, turn and head for the door, putting the mag into my jacket, zipping it up and exiting hastily. I excluded the chemists from my choice of outlets, but remembered that the Queens Head pub, which we had occasionally been to for our basket meals, had a condom machine in the men's toilets. One afternoon I cycled on my tradesman's bike to the pub, leant it up against the outside wall and went inside where I purchased an orange juice, then I entered the toilets and hastily fed the machine with coins before anyone came in, then back in the bar I finished my drink and cycled home. When I confessed to Sara that I had condoms, it was like I had discovered a secret key, which unlocked a valuable treasure, the key to her body! We both had a liking for classical music and would make love whilst Ravel's Bolero was playing on the record player, a piece that lasted 15 minutes and 50 seconds!

MOVING ON

I continued signing on for unemployment into spring 1981, when an advert for a cigarette company caught my eye. Gallaher in Northolt were looking for drive team trainees, so after being interviewed I was offered a position on 15th April, subject to a medical. Having a medical seemed like standard practice in the 80s, but not something that seems to be around today. I started on 11th May, on a salary of £4,428, with a week's training at the Northolt head office along with five other lads. Sales training took the form of standardising the method of selling, repetitive sequences of vocabulary that allowed you to follow a path to the close of sale. We were taught the 4Ps, a sequence of selling any product, whether it was a packet of cigarettes, a fountain pen, or a box of matches.

1. Pack – describe the packet, colour, size etc.
2. Product – discuss the merits of the product, the quality etc.
3. Price – advise on the costs, profits etc.

4.   Plusses – talk about the benefits of the product, promotions like TV advertising etc.

Attached to the training room was a mock shop, set up just like a newsagent, with a counter full of stock and a cigarette gantry behind. A camera was trained on the scene which fed live pictures back to the training room where the proceedings could be watched by the other trainees. We each took turns to enter the 'shop' carrying a little black briefcase which contained two cigarette brands. The trainer would pretend to be the shopkeeper, and we were to sell the brands to him. This felt terrifying, I was as nervous as hell, especially knowing everyone was watching. Occasionally something funny would happen. Part of the sales process was to get behind the counter to merchandise the stock you had sold, but the trainer would say he had a ferocious dog at his feet and then make barking noises. You could hear loud laughter coming from the other room. The trainer would intentionally throw you off your stride, hoping you could recover and get to the sales close. Overall, the method was sound, you knew where you were going, and where you should end up.

Drive team was a method of increasing product distribution in any area. The team, in this case, five lads, would spend the week in a hotel in any part of the country and blitz the areas' retail outlets selling the drive lines. These were the brands that the company wanted to increase in distribution. The stock was secreted in the back of your car covered by a tarpaulin, in our case, a Mini Metro. The downside to this position was that you had to be at the hotel by the Sunday evening, which meant, depending on your location, leaving home on the Sunday afternoon. Our first boss, or team leader as they were known, was Chris, a hardnosed Portsmouth fan. He was out to trip you up, catch you out, and give you a dressing down at any opportunity. We were targeted on the number of calls we made each day, the percentage of sales in those calls, and whether the sales were to new stockists. If any merchandising was done, we would claim how much we had put up, and whether we had stuck any advertising either on the windows, door, or gantry. We were given a Phillips red book street map of the area and told to cover certain pages. This was done in the following way. At your start point, you drive forward and take the second left turn, then left, left, and left again which brings you back to where you started. You then repeat the process ad infinitum, this ensures that you drive down every street, calling into every possible retail outlet on the left-hand side of the road. If you are driving and you see a shop on the right-hand side, you ignore it because you will pass it on the next circular route. Public houses were included and if they were closed you made a note of its position on the map and return later when it was open. When we called on pubs, we would carry in a plain cardboard box which would contain a display unit made up with different cigars. After placing the box on the counter, you would then talk about the cigarette brands. In those days cigarette vending machines were sparse and pubs sold individual packs of cigarettes over the counter. If the publican asked what was in the box, you would say 'I'll get to that later'. After continuing on about the cigarettes, and repeatedly ignoring their questions about the box, their curiosity was so great that they wanted it regardless of the contents. It made it so much easier to sell. At the end of the day, you returned to the hotel with your call sheet and the money collected from the sales, where you cashed up and replenished your stock. The following day, Chris might take your call sheet from the previous day, along with a map, and retrace your steps, checking if you had missed any calls. He would count the advertising stickers were correct as you had claimed, and any deviation in your claim would put you in trouble.

Life in the hotel consisted of having our evening meal, playing pool if we were lucky enough to have one in the hotel, drinking, or watching television in your bedroom. You always shared a room with a colleague, and depending on the hotel, some of the older ones had rooms for three people. Gallaher were massive sponsors of sporting events and in the summer of 1981, we had to attend the Open Golf Championship at the Royal St George Golf Club in Sandwich, Kent. We were positioned in kiosks around the course selling cigarettes, two people in each one. The weather was glorious and at times I had the opportunity to walk around the course and pick up autographs of the golfers. Some notable autographs include Bernard Gallacher, Greg Norman, Ben Crenshaw, Bernhard Langer, Ray Floyd and Tony Jacklin, along with the radio personality Terry Wogan. Around the course there were exhibitions related to golf, with one displaying large photographs of various golfers. On the final Sunday I managed to blag a large picture of Johnny Miller and armed with this I headed to the final hole where the golfers finished. As Johnny finished putting, he headed for the judge's tent to record his score. They should go directly to the tent before signing autographs, but as I was stood behind numerous children who were asking him to sign their books, I held the picture high and shouted, "Hey, Johnny, can you sign this?" He took one look, strode over, asked me where I got it from, then signed it much to the dismay of the waiting kids. The position of drive team leader was seen as a steppingstone to promotion within the company, so thankfully they changed regularly, and we soon said goodbye to the scheming Chris and welcomed Roger as our leader. Roger was older than us but more fun than Chris.

Along came 1982 and with it some personal changes. We were travelling across the south of England, staying in different hotels, sometimes for two or three weeks at a time. One such place was the Bolney Grange Hotel at Bolney, Sussex. Again, Gallaher was involved in sporting events and very close to the hotel was Hickstead show jumping course. We worked at the course four times that year, selling cigarettes from kiosks. Working at the course was more like a holiday than work, no targets to achieve or selling to do. The mood at the hotel was one of fun. We often went out for a curry at a local restaurant and on one occasion we all jumped into the boss's car, "everyone in" he says, and with that puts the car into reverse, unaware that one of the rear doors was still open and it tore the door off when it hit Barrett's car, damaging them both. At one of these meals, we had managed to entice another guest to join us, a pretty woman who obviously enjoyed the attention. The lads were like bees around a honeypot, trying to impress her. I just sat there watching the proceedings, and after the meal we all went back to the hotel. The lads were all hoping to entice her back to their rooms. Just as I was about to go to bed, she appeared down a back set of stairs, grabbed my hand, and took me to her bedroom. She said she picked me as I was the quiet one! I certainly didn't complain!

The event that changed my life that year was on meeting a young woman who was an air stewardess for Dan Air. We hit it off straight away; being with her, the feeling I had was electric, and I felt ecstatic. I didn't feel any guilt towards Sara. Instead, I made a decision that changed the course of my life.

In April of that year the Falklands war had begun – the Argentinians had taken over the island of South Georgia in the South Atlantic, then proceeded to land on the Falkland Islands. The UK responded by sending a task force of 20,000 troops and a flotilla of warships. Seeing these images on TV had a profound effect on me, especially when HMS Sheffield was destroyed by an Argentinian Exocet missile and sunk, with the loss of 20 servicemen. All this was happening 8,000 miles away, and I felt helpless, but proud of the British troops, and my outlook on life was changing. If incidents like this can happen so suddenly, then I wanted to take every opportunity to live life to the full. I had been with Sara for five years, we had got engaged, had holidays in Portugal, Morocco and Austria and had bought our first house together, a top floor maisonette in Southview Rise for £21,950 which we had planned to move into soon. At the same time, I had been seeing the air stewardess regularly during my stays at the Bolney Grange and made the big decision to tell Sara about it, which led to me breaking up with her. It was such a difficult thing to do, but knowing I had my new relationship to fall back on, it made it easier for me. It was harsh of me to treat her in this way, and totally disrespectful after the time we had been together. In hindsight it was appalling, but I was only thinking about myself. She took the news badly, which was to be expected, and I'm sure Peggy wanted to kill me.

On my last visit down to the hotel at Bolney for the Hickstead work, I went to catch up with the stewardess only to find out that she had been seeing another guy who had been staying at the hotel, and she dumped me! Talk about karma, I didn't see that one coming. The advantage of this break-up was that I didn't have the emotional baggage of a five-year relationship. After things between Sara and I had become less hostile, I contacted her to arrange to meet up. I picked her up and we went to the Horse and Groom pub in Alresford, where we discussed what to do with various items that we had bought together over the years, and to discuss the maisonette that we had bought together. We didn't have any furniture in the rooms as we hadn't moved in yet. We agreed that I would buy her out and own it outright myself. I also told her what had happened with the air stewardess and that we were not together anymore. We spent an agreeable evening together, but, unknown to me, sat at the table next to us listening in, was my future wife!

I continued working at Gallaher on drive team and in 1983 we were sent to South Wales to stay in a hotel at Chepstow. The Silk Cut Masters golf tournament was taking place, and in the week prior, we spent our time calling around all the local golf clubs making sure that Silk Cut cigarettes were stocked and to deliver free of charge merchandise such as parasols, bar mats, playing cards and cribbage boards. Come the time of the tournament we were again positioned in kiosks around the course. ITV were covering the event for television, and I was asked to take the trophy to them to feature on TV. Carrying the trophy, I was collected by a woman who took me to a tall gantry built by the 18th green, where I climbed up to the top to find the presenter Steve Rider and a TV camera. According to the cameraman, Steve was very nervous as this was one of his first live links on TV. The woman asked me about the history of the trophy. "I have no idea; I was only asked to deliver it," I replied. In his live link Steve was talking so loud that he had shouts from the golfers on the green below to keep the noise down. A young Welsh golfer called Ian Woosnam won the tournament.

I spent two and a half years on drive team arriving every Sunday and heading home Friday lunchtime. I believe my habit of drinking on a Sunday stems from this time. I hated having to report to work on what was still the weekend, and my way of coping was to drink. I recall one morning following a bit too much alcohol, I was in a shop trying to sell the owner some cigarettes when I suddenly felt sick. I asked if he had a toilet I could visit, where I was promptly sick, and then returned to the shop and still managed to get a sale. Our time in the hotels were fun at times, and practical jokes were played all the time. On one occasion at St Catherine's Lodge Hotel in Hove, I heard a knock on the door. Upon opening it, I was faced with a large rectangular-sized table blocking the door, with Roger, our boss, stood behind it, explaining to the hotel manager, who happened to catch him in the act of moving the table, that as he was walking down the corridor he came across this table in the doorway and was trying to return it back to where it belongs! On another occasion at a hotel in the north of England, I turned up late one evening to check in. Having got my room, I went to the bar for a drink before eating. In the bar I met an older Scottish woman, and we struck up a conversation, and as she also hadn't eaten, we decided to eat together. There was an instant attraction and we both knew where we were going to end up, our appetites were suppressed in anticipation. After the meal we headed back to her room where I spent the night. In the morning I returned to my own room where I discovered that my colleagues had decided to play a trick on me and had taken my bed from the room and moved it into another one, only for the trick to backfire on them as I didn't need it!

THE SINGLETS

At the end of November 1983, I was given a permanent territory local to Alton and it was when I was working on this area that Phil came back into my life at a shop in Frensham. He also worked for Gallaher's and he had strayed off his area onto mine and by pure chance we bumped into each other. We had previously worked together on drive team, so we knew each other well. He lived in the west country but had relocated up to Hampshire and was living in Alton. We soon became mates and drinking buddies, spending a lot of time together; he was like a brother to me, and we had similar interests with football, golf, snooker, and women. Along with another mate Andy we used to frequent the pubs of Alton on a Friday or Saturday night hoping to pull, although that never happened when we desperately went looking for it. We also made trips out to other towns, and on one such occasion the three of us had gone to Farnham where we wandered about the pubs. One such pub had the sign 'no singlets' above the door. Of course, we had no idea what this meant. Did it mean if you weren't in a relationship, you couldn't come in? None of us were in relationships, so we were all by definition 'singlets'. Our minds went into overdrive thinking up the different scenarios, and so 'The Singlet Club' was born. We met up at The Hop Poles pub in Alton and decided on who would hold what position. I was made the treasurer, Phil was the chairman and Andy was the secretary. We decided that we would put £3 each per month into the club funds, and I even had an appointment with Nat West bank and explained the plans we had for expansion. I am amazed that they believed my story hook, line, and sinker, and as a result, I opened an account where we initially put £9 in. Comically, £9 was the only money ever put in because we lacked discipline in running it. At the time a further mate, Ian, became the 4th Singlet member. We produced a 'Singlet Club Magazine' on two occasions purely for the amusement of us four Singlets. All the contents were based on our own experiences and were designed to take the mickey out of each other. We all had an input into the content either by writing pieces or designing pages. For instance, we had a Singlet page 3 slot featuring a pornographic photo of a woman with my face stuck over the original face, complete with my moustache, with a quote from 'Martina'. Asked how she prefers her men, Martina replied, "any which way but limp, I can't stand a man who goes limp after a few pints, that's why I hang around with those great young studs the singlets". We had a mystery page designed to reveal which singlet had possession of the singlet medal as it had disappeared. The medal was made and presented to the singlet who pulled the least attractive girl and was currently held by myself but somehow was not in my possession. There were cartoons drawn by singlet Ian depicting the singlet world tour 2033, with each of us drawn how he thought we would look aged in our 70s. There was an advert for a 'Singlet Club Calendar 1991', and I quote:

'See all your favourite members nude! See the members' members, full frontal, up shots, down shots and inside shots. See your favourite pin up 3 times.

Singlet Andy – Feb, Sept, Nov – the shortest possible months, you will see why!

Singlet Martin – Jan, Aug, Dec – for those dark nights and hot sizzling days!

Singlet Phil – Apr, May, Jun – the 3 months with girl's names!

Singlet Ian – Mar, Jul, Oct – the odd months!

Send £3.95 to Singlet Club Calendar offer.'

We also had a Singlet Club financial report detailing the club's finances in the bank, precisely £9 and 58p interest, a crossword with clues linked to our experiences and Poopers Problem Page. We had really taken an idea based on a misunderstood sign above a pub door and run with it, creating a lasting memory which is still remembered today.

MARRIAGE

I went to a fancy-dress party in early '84 near the village of Farringdon dressed as Boy George, with tassels hanging from my hair and wearing a black hat. While I was there my friend Pat came up to me and she was crying. She told me that her boyfriend was with another girl, and she pointed her out to me. "Don't be daft, that's my brother's wife, she's not with him," I said. Sometime later I discovered that it was indeed true. I was also approached by another woman who said, "I know all about you, Martin, and you've got a false tooth as well," she said. I was shocked, who was this person with information about me, and who had pointed out my bridged tooth? Her name was Sandy, she was a dental assistant and she had been sitting on the next table at the Horse and Groom pub when I had met Sara to discuss the future after our break-up. No doubt she had been listening in! We spent some time talking to each other and before she left, she gave me her phone number to ring. She lived at Four Marks with her parents Ron and Jean. Their house was set in considerable grounds with a swimming pool, and Ron ran his building business from a large shed on site. There were other outbuildings as well as a stables where Sandy kept her horse, Rakie, who had access to a large field at the bottom of the premises. Sandy's parents were traditional parents – Ron earnt the money with his building business while Jean ran the house, sorted out meals and laid Ron's clothes out for him in the morning. If she didn't do so, Ron would have no idea where his clothes were kept!

Sandy and I began an intense whirlwind romance, so much so that after just five weeks together we decided we wanted to get married. When we announced this to her parents, Ron said, "Don't worry, Jean, marry at haste, repent at leisure!" I don't recall why we rushed into such a big decision; was it love? Or lust? Or were we just impulsive? I was 25 years old, not exactly wet behind the ears. Sandy and I did have one slight disagreement prior to our wedding. I had given Sandy a key for my maisonette and she found photograph albums of Sara and me in a drawer in my bedroom. She wanted me to destroy them but I took them to my mum's house for safe keeping.

From this point onwards, everything moved at 100 miles per hour. We started to look for somewhere to live and liked a farmworker's cottage in the village of Binsted three miles from Alton, which we purchased for £36,500 as early as the end of May. The maisonette in Southview Rise was put up for sale at £28,995 and the sale was completed on 30th July. Sandy's dad, Ron, leant us £36,000 for the purchase in Binsted until my sale went through to save us paying for a bridging loan. The house in Binsted was at 8 The Street, a semi-detached house named 'Dogsbody'. This was in reference to the previous occupier who was a jack of all trades, master of none. We quickly changed the house name to 'Sandmartins', a play on words of our names and a reference to the local sand martins bird population. The property was accessed up seven steps bordered by metal railings, to the front door. Inside, you entered into a sparse kitchen with a bathroom on the left of the room, then on through into a lounge with an open fire chimney place. Then you turn left up the stairs to three bedrooms, the largest overlooking the rear of the property, which had a 150-foot garden with greenhouse and shed backing onto farmland. The house also came with access to an allotment across the road at the local recreation park. We set about transforming the inside of the property by changing the downstairs bathroom into a kitchen which allowed the kitchen area to become a dining room. Upstairs we moved an internal wall between the front two bedrooms to make a larger second bedroom along with a decent sized bathroom where we installed a corner bath. Sandy's dad had taken on the building work required to make the internal changes, which were completed not long after we were married. The wedding date was set for 8th September, to take place at the Good Shepherd church in Four Marks and then a reception afterwards at Ye Olde Pig and Whistle pub at Privett. We had furnished the rooms throughout the house and moved in directly after the wedding. We still had some DIY jobs to finish, like sanding down the pine slatted walls that had been painted over the years, to bring them back to their former glory. The large garden also needed work doing, and with a greenhouse available, I managed to grow many vegetables from seed to plant on the allotment.

NEW EMPLOYMENT

On a work level, I had run my own area at Gallaher's for nearly 18 months when I became disillusioned with promotion prospects, probably the only time in my work life where I considered promotion. The work was all retail-based, calling on independent and multiple shops; the next step up would have been wholesale and cash-and-carry work, but opportunities were limited. I have no idea why I made this next move because it still involved retail work but I answered an advert for a salesman at a company called Dennison Manufacturing, who had a head office in Watford. They were launching a new brand of computer disks, ribbons, and computer accessories into the UK under the name of Elephant Memory Systems (EMS).

I started my new job on 6th May 1985 on a starting salary of £8,000 plus commissions, with the intention of building a new retail territory from scratch. My area covered Cornwall to Kent, Bristol to Essex and the whole of London. The rest of the country was covered by another colleague based in Todmorden, Yorkshire.

The first consideration I had was to identify the areas that had the most potential, where I would get the most sales. This clearly was going to be London, and more specifically, Tottenham Court Road, renowned for selling electronic goods. I set about regularly travelling to London, walking the streets visiting every retail store to sell EMS. By far, the most popular products were its floppy disks, and I had soon built a base of customers to start earning commission. I also opened up an account at the Virgin Megastore in Oxford Street at the top of Tottenham Court Road. Outside of London, I did the same in the provincial towns around the south, but not to the success I had in the capital.

The following summer, Sandy and I had an opportunity to spend time on holiday with friends, Steve and Anne, and Martyn and Lynne, who both owned a speedboat between them. They were planning to go to Cornwall to partake in water-skiing and camp at Pentewan Sands campsite which bordered the sandy beach. I asked if I could take the week off as a holiday but was told that I could not take it because the rep in the north was off the same week. In those days we did not have any mobile phones, and communication between myself and head office was either by public phone box or post. When I worked in London, I would spend hours looking for a phone box that was working; British Telecom was in a dire state, and phone boxes were either vandalised or fell into a state of disrepair.

Each week I recorded my work call information on an A4 sheet of paper and sent it into head office, so I had no problem when I produced the following plan based on the notion that head office couldn't contact me. My area included the west country so, I thought, why not spend time down there. This way I could have my holiday, do some water-skiing, and fill in a bogus A4 work sheet to send in at the end of the week. What could go wrong? Off we set for Cornwall where we camped, and water skied through the week. However, there was a nagging doubt in the back of my mind which kept appearing in my thoughts. It was my conscience! It had got the better of me so I decided I would pop into St Austell to contact a few retailers, to make myself feel better if nothing else. I found a phone box in town, grabbed the yellow pages, and started ringing a few numbers and recording their responses on my work sheet. All went well until I was on the phone with a customer when a fire engine, with blaring sirens going, went past the phone box. "Where are you?" said the customer, not realising the reason for his question. "I'm at the head office in Watford," I replied. "Are you sure, I can hear the same sirens outside my shop!" he responded. Panicking now, I reiterated, "No, I'm at the head office…so you don't need anything today," I said and hung up quickly. My mind had flashbacks to the Key Markets incident a few years before. It transpired that I was in a phone box outside the computer shop! That embarrassment apart,

I had managed to take a week's holiday without the knowledge of my employers. Fast forward a few months to September and I had notice that I was to be made redundant, again, and my employment would terminate on 1st October. My letter of notice stated that 'it is in no way a reflection on your performance or skills as a sales representative which I believe have been a credit to the company'. Did I feel guilty about my deception in the summer? Did I hell! With hindsight I had made a pre-emptive strike.

Quickly following the redundancy, I contacted a management consultants firm called Illingworth & Associates who had a number of positions on their books. I owe a lot to John Griffin who was my contact, because he taught me how to approach an interview and the tactics to use, so much so that I received three job offers within a two-week period. One of these was at Tobler Suchard, the Swiss chocolate manufacturers. A problem arose when I turned the position down in favour of one of the other job offers, then, changing my mind on John's advice, spoke to Tobler Suchard's managing director who agreed a starting date with me before he promptly went on holiday to Africa. In the meantime, I was asked to attend another interview with Tobler where the interviewer was not aware of this information. He seemed surprised when, as he began the interview in earnest, I told him that I already had the job. I started on 24th November on a salary of £8,600, working a territory in Hampshire and Surrey, and my boss was Colin who lived close by in Fleet. Again, it was retail-based, calling on independents and multiple outlets. My first task working with colleagues was driving a hired Renault Master van around the area delivering chocolate liqueurs into Martins newsagents; liqueurs were very big at the time although their popularity was waning. In the new year I would concentrate on my territory work, where at certain times of the year, selling an Easter or Christmas range was the priority.

BAD TIMES AHEAD

On the home front, Sandy and I had numerous holidays together over the years, including Zante, Crete, and a two-resort holiday in Florida and then on to the Bahamas. We went with Steve, Anne, Martyn and Lynne, and spent the first week visiting the theme parks in Orlando, then travelled down to Miami to catch a flight to Nassau. Following a nervy flight through a thunderstorm on approach to landing, we settled into the hotel for some sunbathing time, and drinking cocktails around the pool. The following day we had a walk around town. Steve, who was born with a smile on his face, inquisitively asked an approaching black man about the large coconut he was carrying. The six of us stood there intently listening to him as he told us how he has to climb the tree, cut down the coconut from the tree and then sell it, doing all this to make a living. At the end of his story, he held out his hand and said, "And that's how I make a living". Without hesitation, Anne dived headfirst into his arms while we stood there dumbfounded, before we realised, she had fainted from too much sun and alcohol the day before. Unfortunately, the guy with the coconut didn't get any tips as we transported Anne back to the hotel.

On 15th October of that year, we went to bed with the words of Michael Fish ringing in our ears. On his earlier weather forecast he started with "Earlier on today, apparently, a woman rang the BBC and said she heard there was a hurricane on the way. Well, if you're watching, there isn't". That night we were awoken by the worst storm to hit the UK for 300 years. The highest gust recorded at Shoreham on the coast hit 120 mph; during the night the tree in the garden was bent double. Stupidly, I decided to go over to my allotment to try to stop the winds destroying my runner bean framework, which was made from a steel bracing building bracket, but soon realised my efforts were futile. In the morning all roads into and out of Binsted were blocked by fallen trees, no-one was able to leave the village, but thankfully there was no major structural damage to the house, although 18 people in total were killed in the UK.

By the end of the year, we had decided that we wanted to be in Alton where there was a new housing estate being built at Weydale Rise, just off Windmill Hill. The last batch of houses were being released, which included the show house, 1 Haydock Close. This was a three-bedroom detached house with a double garage on a corner plot, on sale for £99,950. After some negotiation, they accepted an offer of £93,500 and our house in Binsted was sold for £80,000 to some friends of Sandy's. We exchanged at the end of March and moved in. Sandy worked in Alton for Engelmann & Buckham, a manufacturing machinery supplier, in the sales department. This meant she occasionally made sales trips abroad, during which a colleague would accompany her. Initially it didn't bother me as I had left my jealousy back at college. Christmas came and I gave Sandy an eternity ring for her main present (we would be together forever, wouldn't we?). Sandy's present to me was suitcases (was she trying to tell me something?). I had no idea what was happening in our marriage but it wasn't going in the right direction. Our relationship was faltering, although then I couldn't see why. As a couple we didn't seem to be doing anything together. I had felt aggrieved for some time, that after work she went to her parents' home to tend after her horse, but I needed tending as well. Nothing seemed out of place between us at home, but she started to spend time with characters that were around her when she was younger. I was not accompanying her at these times so when she had to make daily visits to her horse, I had no idea where or who she was with. Looking back, I felt our biggest downfall was communication. We should have discussed how we were feeling about each other, and work out how to get through things, but we just seemed to give up, we made no effort with the marriage at all. We drifted apart and, in the spring, Sandy said she was leaving. It didn't worry me at all, it was a relief in some ways; however, having a failed marriage drove me to drink more than I should have. I had also been advised by the doctor that I had high cholesterol and that I should cut down on consuming fatty food products. I had been prescribed statins at the age of 29 years, and with the thought in my head that my dad died at the age of 35, I spent the next six years suffering from anxiety, fixated on dying early like my dad had done. Remarkably, when I reached the age of 36, the anxiety disappeared completely. I had lived longer than my dad and I had broken the curse. Sandy moved back to her parents after we agreed I would stay in the house, but we would also put the house up for sale.

I continued working at Tobler Suchard, but my home life was affecting my work. The company had various sales trips abroad, notably, to the Alps in Switzerland, and treating these trips like a holiday didn't do me any favours. I liked to have a beer. Colin was a mentor to me, he took me under his wing, and pushed me to improve myself. One such occasion, they were looking for another sales manager, and Colin encouraged me to apply for the position. This involved having a group interview at head office in Bedford, with five other guys. We were asked to set out different tasks and present a subject to the group that you had been briefed on. Also, we undertook tasks like the one where you are on a plane which crashes in the desert, and you can only take three items with you from the wreckage – what are they? Fuck me! Who cares? Ok, I would take a window with me so that when it gets hot I can open it! And I'll take the dune buggy that I packed in a crate in the back of the plane. What? You didn't know I packed one? Well, tough shit, see you later! What the hell were these interviews designed for, to employ the person with the loudest voice? The problem for me was that I had always been a shy lad so sitting in a room full of peers getting them to listen to me would never happen. You had to have the loudest voice, and, in a personal setting, my voice is pretty loud, but in a work environment it takes a back seat. This was my fourth sales position and I had been made redundant from two of them, Findus, and Dennison. At Gallaher I had spent half my time travelling round the country, starting on a Sunday, living in hotels and all the stress that brings, and at Tobler I suffered from a broken marriage. God, I hated work! Work was not a labour of love for me, it was a means to an end, and if I look back at those jobs, I didn't enjoy any of them. I now had ingrained into me a philosophy that said, 'do as little as possible to get by'.

SINGLE AGAIN

O f course, being a single guy again meant I could play the field, and boy, it was a big playing field. Every weekend, I would be out with the singlets, Phil, Ian, and Andy, which began when we met up in the Eight Bells pub, then wandered down to the market square, which had an establishment on every side, then finish up at the Hop Poles (or slop poles as we called it), hoping to pull some young woman, and young some of them were. I was now 29 years old but didn't bat an eyelid if they were only 17. I used the fact that I had a house just up the road from the pub, where we could carry on drinking after the pub closed at 11pm. The singlets liked to play games, board games, and once back at my house, out would come the Trivial Pursuit, which soon became a game of strip Trivial Pursuit – if you got a question wrong, off came a garment! Before long, we would all be naked, spread around on the living room floor, consuming bottles of wine, which incidentally were delivered in error to my house by Tobler, originally intended as promotional gifts, but an order of 72 duplicated bottles arrived which I kept quiet about!

When I lived in Binsted the local pub, The Cedars, was two doors away, and while I didn't use it that often when I lived there, Phil and I would regularly go up to the pub on a Thursday evening. It was run by Terry and Babs. Terry was the archetypal landlord, entertaining the clients, having a drink with them, and being a jolly good host. His drinking over the years had given him a barrel belly, just what you would expect, but it went back a lot further. Terry's best man at his wedding was the great Oliver Reed, well known for his alcoholism and binge drinking. Babs looked after the food side of the business and was a great cook, even winning a national competition for the best gravy.

On the first occasion we started visiting on a Thursday, we joined in a card game where we played blackjack. Stakes were 10p per card, and by the end of the evening the stakes had risen to 50p per card, but never more. When we left that first time, Phil and I counted up our money and found we had both had a profitable night. Our Thursday night visits became a regular occurrence, and we rarely came away losing. However, one Sunday afternoon we visited the pub hoping to play cards, and it turned into the most frightening scenario for me ever! We had been dropped off at the pub, intending to get a taxi home. In those days the pubs had to close on a Sunday afternoon from 3pm, but this was one of those days that Terry was happy to draw the curtains and carry on serving. We'd had a few drinks through the day and started up our usual game of blackjack, 10p per card rising to 50p per card. The dealer stayed as the dealer until they lost the hand and then the dealing went to the winner. The afternoon wore on into the early evening, and a person who we hadn't seen before came into the bar and wanted to join in, which we were happy for him to do. The card stakes went up to £1 per card, then £2, but we happily played along. I had won a hand so became the dealer, and went on to win numerous hands, all the while the stakes per card rose…£5…. £10…. and I kept winning the hands and stuffing the money into my back pocket, even being helped by a local woman to straighten the money out before it went in my pocket…it now became £20 per card. By this time a crowd had gathered around, fascinated by the proceedings. We were approaching the end of the evening, and having had quite a bit to drink, I stated that I would hold five more hands and then I must go home. The five hands came, and I kept winning, I'd never seen a run of winning hands like this ever before, but I kept putting the money in my pocket, until the five hands were dealt. "Right, that's it, we're going," I said. "Just one more hand," the stranger stated, so I dealt one more hand. The stranger, after seeing his first card said, "I'll go a monkey", my mate Phil went £200 (on an IOU to me) and Jamie went £80. I dealt the second card without even understanding what a monkey was, and again I heard "I'll go a monkey". Phil went £200 again and Jamie £80. I looked at my cards, twisted another card, and lost! The stranger said, "Do you know what a monkey is?" – "no," I replied. "It's £500, you owe me £1,000," he said. I slipped off the barstool backwards, and thought, 'what the fuck have I done, don't tell me this is real, how am I going to pay this'. Slowly, I came to my senses, pulling the money from my back pocket, and straightening it out. I started counting, £100, £200, £300… £600, £700… I kept going and when I finished counting I had £2,000 in my pocket. I had lost £1,560 in one hand and still had change left! However, as we were arranging a taxi the stranger insisted he would give us a lift home to Phil's house in Alton, which he did. Once there, he again insisted he come in and we continue playing cards, telling me I still had a wad of money left. Reluctantly we agreed, and he slowly started winning, all the while telling me the same thing, that I had a wad of money left. Eventually, I said it had all gone but he didn't believe me. Even so I packed up and walked home, with £80 left. After this experience, I struggled to sleep at night, re-running the events over in my mind, thinking of how close I had come to a financial disaster. I never ever gambled like this again, my lesson had been learnt.

Sandy and I had put the house up for sale and we eventually found a buyer. A sale for £119,000 was agreed, and with a completion date in sight Sandy came round to the house so that we could agree on how to divide up the contents. As we went around the house, I had a clipboard in my hand with a line drawn down the middle of the page, my name on the left side, Sandy's name on the right. We went from room to room and I noted who was having what item. It was such an amicable way to behave, I'm sure there are many married couples who wished their marriage split up was as amicable as ours. "You have the washing machine; I'll have the cooker" was typical of the conversation that day. I was even able to store my belongings from the house in Sandy's dad's outbuildings.

When completion day came, I moved out and returned to my mum's house where I lived until early 1990. I still worked for Tobler Suchard, but I was starting to consider my future options. I had money in the bank and I didn't have a mortgage, so what did I need a job for? Early that new year I made a decision. I'm going to give up my job and travel around Europe. If I didn't do it now, I might regret that decision for the rest of my life. I don't want to get to 40 or 50 years old and wish I had done it. It was a brave decision, but it was for my sanity as well. I'd always been happy with my own company, and making brave decisions took me back to the choice I had made as a nine-year-old. It was for my own good. I set about planning my adventure. I wanted a Volkswagen camper van, and I found a business near Bishops Waltham that restored camper vans. I went down to the garage and saw an orange and white VW

T2 version, which had been restored to a high standard. I snapped it up for a price of £6,000, put my notice in and left work in April of that year. The camper had an extending roof which you unclipped and pushed up, to give extra standing height. There was a removeable table attached under the window with seating either side and a soft cushioned seat that stretched across the width of the van which turned into a double bed. By the door stood the cooker, which, when unhooked swung around to the outside so you could cook alfresco, and opposite the cooker was a fridge. In the roof were two pull-out hammock beds, enabling four people to sleep in total.

Over the previous two years I had made the acquaintance of a young French girl called Roxanne; she was about five feet two inches tall, had red hair and a gallic appearance. She had lived in England for a few years but wanted to return to Paris, where her family lived. I agreed that when I headed off abroad she could come with me; this would enable her to pack all her belongings in the back of the van, and as a thank you to me, I could stay at her parents' for a week before heading off on my own.

MY TRAVEL DIARIES

The departure date was set for Monday 21st May. The Sunday was spent with Amanda and Tess. Amanda was Sandy's friend from work, whom I got along with well. We went to the Hop Poles and met up with other friends which enabled me to say goodbye to them all. On the Monday morning I went to Mum's to say goodbye before picking up Roxanne and heading off to Portsmouth where we were catching the ferry. I felt sad to be leaving Alton, and my eyes filled with tears listening to Enya on a tape. "Are you alright?" asked Roxanne, but I struggled to answer as tears again welled up. I had recovered by the time we got to the ferry, only to realise I had not signed my passport so got questioned by customs. We boarded virtually last, but somehow were directed past all the parked vehicles to end up at the bow of the ship.

Tuesday 22nd May

After a restless night sleeping in the bar, we awoke at 6am, and docked at 7am, then we headed to the van. We were the second motor off, and after passing through passport control, I headed for the streets of Le Havre. Once on the correct road we headed for Rouen, then stopped at Gaillion for breakfast, a ham sandwich and coffee for 33 francs. Roxanne was navigating but she wasn't very good, so I pulled over in a layby to check the map myself. Having done so, I decided I wanted a wee, so I headed for the wood nearby and returned to the van. We had driven 50 yards when I started to smell dogshit, and realised my shoes were caked in it. I jumped out and used half a box of tissues trying to clean them off; meanwhile Roxanne found it all very amusing. I reckoned this was human shit which made me feel sick, but I did the best job I could cleaning them before driving off. However, I could still smell them even though I had sprayed them with deodorant, so I stopped again and duly left my trusty old shoes on the side of the road watching me drive off in a cloud of dust. We had reached Paris when I discovered Roxanne didn't know where her family lived! We eventually found her parents' flat, and I met her brother Ronan. I introduced myself as Kristof (Christopher) as Martin is a woman's name – at least that's what Roxanne told me – and they didn't need another excuse to laugh at me. My French was not good, and I felt apprehensive about it. Roxanne and I had a sleep for a couple of hours, before I popped to a local shop to get some dinner. Roxanne set me some French translation to help me learn but to no avail. As we sat on the settee, I observed that the apartment was decorated with ornate, tasteful furniture, with a leather corner piece settee and a picture wallpaper making it feel as if you are sitting in a greenhouse looking into the garden. Roxanne's mum was away until Thursday so I would meet her then.

Wednesday 23rd May

At the base of the tower block there is a swimming pool, ice rink and a bowling alley. Roxanne and I had a morning swim in the 100m pool, where I managed 10 lengths in total. The changing rooms are mixed sex and I noticed in the cubicles in the corner of each tile, there were holes drilled through enabling peep holes to look into another cubicle, presumably drilled by young boys hoping to sneak a view of a naked body. The urinals were also open plan so while I stood having a wee, females were wandering by! Roxanne and I went by metro to the Champs-Élysées and walked to the Pont Alexandre III bridge and back again. In the evening we had a couple of games at the bowling alley. I won both of them by quite a lot, and Roxanne was so annoyed by this that she decided to only speak to me in French for the rest of the day, my punishment for her inabilities!

Thursday 24th May

With the shutters down in the bedroom I didn't wake up until 12 noon. We took the metro to the Arc de Triomphe and then walked to the Eiffel Tower. Roxanne hates tourist attractions but I had never been to the top before, so against her will she queued up with me to go up, which took 25 minutes to the top. The evening was spent at Roxanne's friend Valerie's mother's house, where we had a meal. They have a small dog who is very boisterous, so Roxanne and I took it for a walk. I threw the dog's toy while Roxanne was holding the lead and she was pulled over and scratched her hands and elbows, which of course was my fault! Roxanne's mum and stepfather returned from their holiday.

Saturday 26th May

I went for a swim in the morning with Ronan and his girlfriend Aline, and managed 17 lengths. When I first met Aline, she said she didn't speak English; however, I find out she had spent 18 months in Uxbridge working as a receptionist. She said she had felt shy conversing in English. After a six-course lunch I drove Roxanne and her mum to her friend's house 25km north of Paris where we met Dominique and his wife and two kids. When Dominique saw my camper van (affectionately called 'the love shack') he wanted me to take his house and family in exchange for 'le cabane d'amour', which I politely declined as I knew how expensive a wife and two kids can be! In the evening Dominique lit a barbecue and cooked filet mignon, which was superb.

Tuesday 29th May

Today I leave Paris and Roxanne, and head off on my journey around France. After I had bought a bottle of champagne as a thank you to Roxanne's mum, I said goodbye at 11.40am and I headed out of Paris aiming for Chartres by a non-motorway route. I stopped in Chartres for lunch and a look around the cathedral, which was full of English schoolchildren. I headed on towards Chateaudun, which is a magnificent sight as the town is perched on the top of a plateau. After buying refreshments in town, I headed for the campsite and parked up next to the river Loir, listening to the sounds of grasshoppers, birds twittering, cows mooing and fish jumping in the river. After eating I had a stroll around the town, which is on a comparison to Alton for population, but I only saw one bar open, and that was empty. I have driven 95 miles today and the campsite cost 11F.

Wednesday 30th May

I didn't leave the campsite until noon, but deciding not to travel too far today, I headed for Vendome and then onto Blois where I paid 20F for the night. My route will now follow the river Loire until I reach the coast.

Thursday 31st May

It is a lovely warm day today, but when I paid at reception I stupidly said 'bonjour' when I left! I headed for Tours on the N152 on the north bank of the river, which spans 200 yards across at this point. I got lost in Tours looking for the campsite and even drove through a road closed sign, over the roadworks and out the other side – nothing was going to stop the 'love shack'. Miraculously I found the site, which had a swimming pool, a shop, bar, and tennis courts; however a cost of 37F for one night meant I would be paying for facilities that I probably wouldn't use. In the morning an English neighbour came over to complain that my music was too loud for her seven-year-old son who was still sleeping at 10am!

The next few days are spent at campsites in Saumur and Gennes. The Saumur site is located on a long island in the river Loire, which is very pleasant, but I was starting to miss some company; I needed someone to talk to. By luck I had a pleasant evening on the Friday spent talking to my Irish neighbours once they had put their four kids to bed.

Monday 4th June

After a good early start, I arrived at the Atlantic Ocean at a pretty fishing village called Pornic about lunchtime. The harbour is surrounded by small restaurants with tables and chairs spread out before them. I found a site called La Madrague which was perched up high on a hill overlooking the sea. At 6pm I had a stroll along the coast path towards Pornic; at every point a small beach with golden rust brown sand appeared, which was the pattern all along the path. It was about three miles into town, so after suitable refreshment I returned to the site via the road.

Tuesday 5th June

I headed into Pornic to get fuel and was at the garage when I was accosted by an old man who had a letter in his hand. It was written in French and English, and he wanted to know what 'moving the goalposts' meant. It transpires that he had sold his house to a couple who were now divorcing, and they could not settle on an amount between them to share belongings. I headed south on the coast until I reached St Jean-de-Monts, a vast long sandy beach fronted by high rise blocks, holiday villages awaiting the throng of tourists for the holiday season.

Saturday 9th June

Today I nearly had a head-on smash with a car. I was looking for a nice sandy beach and seeing a car park in a wood on the other side of the road, I swung the van around to drive back towards it. However, I totally forgot to drive on the right-hand side, and was faced with an English car coming around a bend, straight for me. Luckily it was English, because the natural instinct is to swerve left, which we both did, I went onto the left-hand side of the road while he took a swerve into what would be oncoming traffic, except luckily nothing was coming. This really shook me up as I thought I had mastered driving on the right.

The coming days are spent at campsites close to the beach, where I managed to get quite a bit of nude sunbathing in. At a beach just north of Montalivet, there was a nudist camp that bordered the beach, so I stayed in the shade to protect my burnt bits, while the beach was busy. Most of the nudists are old men and oversized women, but wait, what's this? Two young girls are setting their towels in front of me, are they going naked?... no…she's got her bikini on… wait…the other one's topless…bottomless! Both of them are naked, so without hesitation, I wander naked towards the sea, past them, my Walkman gently playing, trying to impress them without being locked up for an unwanted erection!

Tuesday 19th June

I awoke to heavy rain, thunder and lightning, and a damp feeling due to having left the roof ventilation open all night. I left the site and progressed around the Arcachon basin, a vast inlet of sea, and then on to Dune de Pilat, the biggest sand dune in Europe. It stretches along the coast for five miles and at its highest is 114 metres high. Negotiating the children on school outings, I walked up the steep wooden steps along the back edge and onto the top. Here, you find yourself looking south along a vast desert, where I walked about a mile to the highest point and sat looking out to sea at the small islands, listening to the shrill screech of a colony of birds.

Tuesday 26th June

I arrived at Biarritz on Sunday afternoon and booked into Biarritz Camping, a site predominantly full of young people, where I met another VW K reg camper van driven by four New Zealand guys touring Europe. They were leaving today to head towards Pamplona for 7th July to see the bull run. I also met an English couple called George and Kate, whom I spent time with in the bar watching the World Cup games. This afternoon my van was parked at a beachside car park, and when I returned I found that I had received a parking ticket. The police were discouraging camper vans from parking near the beach, so apparently I needed to pay 75F for stamps at a newsagent and post them to the police, but I decided not to bother as I will be entering Spain soon. After meeting the New Zealand guys this morning, I decided that I would also head for Pamplona in time to attend the running of the bulls.

Wednesday 27th June

This morning I had planned to check out and move on; however, as I aim for the phone box I meet a young American girl called Liz whom I had offered a drink to the previous night. She had been in France for seven months already and worked in the evening at a pizza restaurant. We got along really well, and she invited me to join her and two cars full of French people heading to the Museum of the Sea. The afternoon was spent wandering around the building before Liz had to go to work. I decided to stay longer as I liked her company.

Thursday 28th June

I had invited Liz for a coffee before lunch, but as she had to attend an interview in town, we put her bike in the van and I took her to the meeting. We agreed a meeting point for afterwards, and I attended early and waited with her bike. However, she came running along the road, so pleased to see me as she had been waiting in a different place. She had nearly 'lost all faith in humanity' thinking that I had stolen her bike. We went back and bought food for the evening for me to cook. It is amazing how kind people can be to one another. After she had attended a babysitting interview, she rushed back and told me the story of a Swedish girl who had arrived after 27 hours on a train from Sweden with nowhere to stay, so Liz had offered her the use of her tent, and I agreed Liz could have my bed while I slept in a bunk above. The next morning, I said goodbye to Liz and crossed into Spain, camping at San Sebastian.

Sunday 1st July

At the campsite I had met a German guy called Bernard, so this afternoon, he, myself, and a guy called Paul took the bus into San Sebastian to watch the football in the old part of town. They also met up with old acquaintances from previous years, three Aussies and three Dutch people, and we all partied through the evening before heading back at 4am!

Wednesday 4th July

I spent some time on San Sebastian beach sunbathing. The beach is sandy and set in a natural cove, protected by the Isle de Santa Clara which is situated in the centre of the bay. If you wander out into the shallow sea, it's not long before you are surrounded by large fish, swimming between your legs. As the tide comes in, sunbathers have to keep moving backwards, until everyone is on top of each other. In the evening I caught the bus into the old part of town where I met previous acquaintances, Anthony, and Pete (an American girl). Pete and I decided to swop clothes, and I ended up topless wearing a skirt. It was here that I met Jessica and Petra, two Swedish girls. I got on very well with Jessica – my drunkenness and cross-dressing habit didn't dissuade her from liking me – and as it was late and I was stuck in town, I went back with the girls to their accommodation where Jessica sneaked me in and kept me warm until morning time.

Thursday 5th July

In the morning I headed by bus back to the campsite where I paid up and then returned back into town to pick up Jessica and Petra in San Sebastian. They had wanted a lift to Pamplona and I agreed they could come with me. Just outside of Pamplona there was a free camp full of campervans, but we could see it was also full of pissed up Aussies and Kiwis. There was also a long queue to enter, so I decided against staying there and headed back to town where I parked in a central car park. We then spent the evening socialising in the old town, and at 3am we headed back to the van where Petra slept in a bunk and Jessica slept with me.

Friday 6th July

Today the Festival of San Fermin begins in the Plaza de Castille at 12 noon. We arrived at 11.50am to be greeted by thousands of people, adults, and children, all dressed in traditional dress of white top, white trousers, a red waist sash and red neckerchief. At 12 noon fireworks signal the start of the festival and to the sounds of bands playing traditional music, everyone dances, champagne spraying over everybody, soaking all in their way. The day is spent drinking, eating and socialising, until the early hours of the morning.

Saturday 7th July

The bull run starts at 8am, so we had an early start to claim our vantage place for the run, the top of a toilet block. At 6.50am it was already three-deep, but the longer we stayed, the nearer to the front we got. We looked down on a street full of nervous runners, and at 8am a cannon sounded, and the gates were opened to release the bulls. We were 500 yards from the start, but already some runners were anxiously moving forward. Within 90 seconds the first bulls arrived and everyone scattered, falling over, jumping onto the side fences, into doorways, anywhere to avoid the bulls. In no time the bulls had passed and were heading for the bullring, and the spectacle was over. In the afternoon we managed to get showers in the public facilities before returning to the van. I asked Jessica if we could get some time alone as Petra had been by her side constantly, and I needed to know her feelings towards me. We had one and a half hours' chat in the park together which I was grateful for. We exchanged addresses and agreed to keep in contact; we were glad that we had met each other. I felt privileged to have done so as I was the one who kissed her, cuddled her, caressed her, stroked her, massaged her, ran my fingers through her hair, and slept next to her, and equally delightful, she returned everything to me. Jessica and Petra set off for Barcelona on the late train, and after attending the nightly fireworks display at the castle, I met up with Fiona, Kathy and Sophie in the Aussie area; the narrow streets were full of rubbish and broken glass inches deep under your feet. Sophie and I bought two bottles of sparkling wine to celebrate Kathy's 25th birthday and we returned to spray them over Kathy at midnight. Beautifully and romantically, two men, one with a trumpet and one with a trombone, passed by and played 'Happy Birthday' to her.

Monday 9th July

I bought a ticket for the bullfight from Tim, a Canadian I had befriended. We went to the bullring in the evening, and boy, what an event it was. The bulls that run through the streets in the morning are slaughtered in the bullring in the evening. As a spectacle, seeing the bulls killed wasn't pleasant, but the experience in the crowd was fantastic; spectators had brought large plastic tubs full of sangria and cooked chicken pieces. These are not drunk or eaten but are thrown at everyone and everybody, drink and food flying through the air; it was such a fantastic time, the bullfights become incidental! After the bullfights we all jumped down into the ring and as numerous bands march out through the exit we all followed and danced to the music along the streets.

Tuesday 10th July

I was up early to get a vantage point just before the tunnel entrance into the bullring, where I crouched down behind the temporary fences erected to protect the crowds. As the bulls passed by, I slipped through and joined the run, through the tunnel into the ring. I wasn't aware that you are not allowed to do this; however, once in the ring along with hundreds of other runners, my adrenaline was flowing fast. A cow is then let into the ring to entice the bulls away through an exit, and then a young steer with horns enters. It soon becomes apparent that standing around looking for the steer becomes impossible, as the first time you are aware it is there is when everyone in front of you scatters, leaving you exposed to being knocked over. Trying to avoid it, I jumped onto the fence and fell over backwards. After all the excitement of the morning, I returned to the Plaza de Castille square, and a bar that we all used to meet up at, where we all told our stories of the run. We sat drinking Zoco, a Spanish liqueur made from sloe berries, coffee and vanilla in an anise flavoured spirit. As the morning passed into afternoon, I became pretty drunk, to the extent that I ended up asleep in the gutter. Kim, an Australian friend, took me back to my van where I slept until 9pm, then I decided to get up and return to the square to continue drinking. Unfortunately, it was a repeat performance: I was asleep in the gutter! When I awoke I headed towards my van, but I struggled to stand up between two parked cars and collapsed in the street. I was picked up by the Red Cross (Cruz Roja) and put into a bed for a while, where I received an injection in my arse of some sort. I also lost my van keys in all the drunkenness but luckily had a spare ignition key in my wallet. Phew!

Wednesday 11th July

A very quiet day today, no drink at all! I Met everyone in the square and regaled them of my adventure the night before. I went to the evening fireworks with Sarah and Ed, two Americans, and as Ed wanted to continue the evening, Sarah came back to the van with me where we slept together, purely platonic, to recharge our batteries.

Thursday 12th July

I woke Sarah up at 7am and we quickly dressed and walked to the square. Ed was running this morning, so Sarah and I found a vantage point to observe the proceedings. Ed got trampled on by a young bull, much to the delight of the crowd! After the run, as Ed and Sarah were heading to France on their travels, I drove them to Tolosa where they found a hotel, and I travelled on to a campsite at Mungia, which was close to Bilbao airport as Ian was arriving at 7.30pm for a two-week stay. Ian's flight did not arrive until 10pm, and he failed to recognise me when he arrived, mainly due to my long hair, bronze tan, and red bandana that I had wrapped around my forehead.

Friday 13th July

We left early morning and headed into Bilbao to find a garage where I could get a new key cut for the van, but couldn't find one, so we headed straight on back to Pamplona. As soon as we got there we headed for the lost property office where I explained that I had lost my keys, and to my shock, they turned out a box full of keys. There must have been 200 sets, probably dating back many years, but my keys weren't there. We spent the afternoon playing football with all the guys and some local kids who ran rings around us, then later went to the evening fireworks display before having a few rides at the fun fair. Later I took Ian to the street of 1,000 bars where we danced until 3.30am.

Saturday 14th July

I was awake by 7am, and after trying to wake Ian unsuccessfully I went to the square and met Anthony, Andy, and Tim. I decided I was going to run today, the last day, so having grabbed a newspaper and rolled it up in readiness to fend off the bulls (are you kidding me, a newspaper!), I waited in the square by the town hall, at the front of the runners. Just before 8am the police broke their cordon and let us move forward. I was extremely anxious as I heard the cannon fire at 8am. I kept looking behind me constantly as I moved forward with the runners, I had to make sure I got through the tunnel into the bullring before the bulls got there. You do not want to be in there with them charging at you, there is nowhere to hide, so I made sure I was down Estafeta and into the bullring about 20 seconds before the bulls came charging through. Once the bulls were out of the ring, the young bulls were released, and this time, I made a beeline towards them, managing to whack them with my newspaper a few times. The whole experience was so exhilarating, my adrenaline was pumping, and I had a great sense of achievement and so glad I took part. Over the whole week Channel 4 had been filming a programme on the bull run, and the bar that we all sat at daily was featured regularly. I managed to catch the programme on my return to the UK later in the year, it was called 'For Whom the Bull Tolls', a play on words from the famous Ernest Hemingway book. On the TV programme I spotted myself running into the bullring followed by the bulls, wearing my mustard-coloured T-shirt which stood out amongst the white tops. Afterwards I returned to the van to wake Ian and at 1pm we left Pamplona to head back to the campsite at San Sebastian. In the evening we headed to Bilbao airport where we picked up Phil, who was coming out for one week.

Sunday 15th July

Today we headed for Laredo and arrived at 1.30pm. We spent the afternoon on the beach. About 100 yards away from us was a kiosk on the sand selling cold drinks. I took Ian's order for a coke and Phil's order for a Seven Up and headed over. The guy saw my red bandana wrapped around my head and said "Ah, San Fermin Festival? Has ido a Pamplona?" to which I replied "Si, dos coca-cola, uno Seven Up". He bent over into the fridge and rummaged around before pulling out two cans of coke and…a Seven Up? He handed me the cans.

Wait a moment, call that a Seven Up? I paid and returned walking across the sand, looking at this can that was covered in rust with the print faded away, my laughter getting louder and louder the closer I approached them, until I cried tears as I handed Phil his drink. He didn't seem amused because Ian joined in the fun. We left the beach to book in at Camping Laredo. After some food, we hit the old town and found the busy bars. After leaving a bar with a bottle of beer under my shirt, the bottle slipped out and smashed on the ground. As I started to walk away, two armed policemen carrying machine guns approached me, and with one shake of their gun towards the smashed glass on the ground, I quickly picked it all up and placed it in a bin. At 2am we went to a disco but as there were no buses or taxis we walked back to the site with some Swedish guys who were also at the same camp and got to bed by 6.30am.

Monday 16th July

At 11.20pm, after an evening meal we went to the Boxer Bar where we noticed three girls we had spoken to the night before, and after introductions by Hemanay, 19-year-old Sonie had her tongue down my throat, kissing me vigorously. Apparently she had been talking about me from the previous day and thought I looked like Kevin Costner!

Tuesday 17th July

We met the girls again this evening, Sonie and I continued where we had left off the night before, Hemanay seemed to be getting on well with Phil, and Ian was getting on well with Mamay. The girls had to leave briefly, advising us that they would be returning to the bar at 12.30am. In the meantime, we returned to camp. Ian and I returned to the bar at 12.30am but Phil stayed at the van as he had thought the arranged meeting time was for 12.30 tomorrow lunchtime. When we met the girls and explained Phil's absence it put paid to any hopes of progress, and the night fizzled out.

Thursday 19th July

We packed up and headed for Santander, where we had lunch at a seafront restaurant. On returning to the van, we discovered it had been broken into and ransacked. Two cameras were stolen, and clothes and my passport were strewn across the floor. The afternoon was spent at the police station giving a statement and filling out forms. Afterwards, we booked into Cabo Major campsite, but the whole theft affair had put a dampener on the day.

Friday 20th July

We stopped at Orinon beach, where Ian and Phil started chatting up this girl called Clare who spent the afternoon with us on the beach, before we discovered that she was only 13 years old! This was definitely not in the Singlet handbook!

Saturday 21st July

We were up early to take Phil to the airport and afterwards Ian and I decided to head back to San Sebastian where we sat on the beach all afternoon. He taught me to play a card game that was based on Trumps. After starting with seven cards, each subsequent round is one card fewer until you get to one card each. You then start to increase each hand by one card until you are back at seven cards. All the while, you score on each round by predicting how many hands you will win. A correct prediction gives you 10 extra points. Ian did not tell me what the name of the game was. After we checked in at Camp Oliden we spent the evening in the bar where we met two German girls and invited them back to the van for further drinks, which lasted until 5am.

Tuesday 24th July

This evening I met Ruth, Lisa, and Cait for the first time, three Australian girls who were staying in San Sebastian. As we were going to be heading to Bilbao tomorrow, Ian and I offered to give them a lift at 5pm the following day, not really expecting them to turn up, but they did. You might think we were generous in our offer, but truth be told, this was in the Singlet handbook Rule 1: 'always say yes to girls'!

Wednesday 25th July

We met the Aussie girls on time and drove to Bilbao but didn't get to the campsite until 9pm. The girls were apprehensive about where they could stay that night, so I offered them to stay in the van as I had room. We all spent the evening drinking a bottle of vodka, singing, and laughing, where eventually Ian and Lisa took the bunks, Cait slept with me on the double bed, and Ruth slept outside on the camp bed.

Thursday 26th July

It was an early start to get to the airport to drop Ian off for his flight home, and by chance we just made it by 9.35am for his flight at 9.50am. I decided that I was happy for the girls to continue travelling with me on my way to Portugal, so we headed west. By the time we had got to Torrelavega the oil light had lit up on the dashboard. By pure chance, I found a VW garage who changed the oil for me. Opening the engine casement was difficult as I had lost the key in Pamplona, but I managed to access the engine from under the seating. We stayed at Ribadesella and that night Ruth slept next to me.

Saturday 28th July

We crossed into Portugal from Spain at 5pm, 4pm in Portugal and stopped at a campsite in Viana Do Castelo, where Wrongy (Lisa's nickname) cooked a pasta meal before we hit the bar. Four beers cost 320 Escudo which equates to £1.20 – it was cheap in northern Portugal. It was Cait's turn to have the comfy bed next to me.

Monday 30th July

After a very drunk Sunday we headed to Porto and arrived by late afternoon. It is such a beautiful city, split in two by the river Douro, and spanned by three bridges built upon high banks. That night at the campsite, the girls hired a caravan to stay in while I slept in my van adjacent to them.

Tuesday 31st July

Most significant action today was that Ruth and Cait decided to cut my hair, although they didn't do a great job. I gave Cait a back massage, probably recommended by Ruth after I gave her the same the previous evening. I did not drink alcohol today!

Thursday 2nd August

We arrived at Nazaré by 8pm and booked into camp Vale Paraiso, squeezing in between two other campers. We cooked up a meal and drank four bottles of wine between us before thumbing a lift at 11pm into town where we sat in the Beach Bar conversing with the locals. We then headed for a disco at 2am where we stayed until 4.30am before hitchhiking back to the camp.

Friday 3rd August

Cait slept next to me last night which was a big mistake for her. During the night in my sleep, I had an attack of cramp in my leg (which they all thought was a heart attack) and I rolled over and laid on top of her, refusing to budge, and then apparently I got rather stroppy with them all! After breakfast we left the site by foot and jumped in the first passing car which dropped us at the beach where we stayed for a while. The town is cornered on the north by a large mountain that projects out into the sea, the beach then runs south towards the port. Out to sea a band of fog stretched from the fort on the mountain to the port, but left the beach bathed in sunshine. A sudden wind direction change brought the temperature plummeting by 10 degrees, although still warm enough to stay, until the fog took off to sea and the sun shone again. We decided to head back to the camp but were unable to gain a lift from anyone and had to walk the whole way back.

Saturday 4th August

After breakfast we waited outside the gates of the campsite to hitch a lift, when a car driven by two German guys stopped and picked us all up and dropped us at the beach. The two guys were from Cologne and their names were Fibbes and Oliver. In the afternoon I sat in the bar with them where we discussed football until the girls joined us from the beach. Today I was feeling a greater detachment from the girls, they seemed to be secretive amongst themselves, making me feel like an outcast; I guess I should think about moving on alone. I felt an instant connection with Fibbes and Oliver, and we spent the evening in town at the Beach Bar before going to a nightclub, where we stayed until 3am. The Aussie girls split up, Ruth disappeared alone and Cait fell asleep in the car until we all met up later to return together.

Sunday 5th August

I woke up late to find the girls had showered and then left for the beach without me, suggesting they would meet up later. Fibbes and Oliver came to the van and we then went to the beach and played cards, but as expected, the girls did not show up. We then decided to drive back to the campsite at 6.30pm; however the traffic was only moving slowly, so Fibbes and I walked next to the car having a laugh while Oliver drove. It took one hour to return, where we then found the girls laid on beds by the van having already eaten a roast chicken. We returned to the town for food, but Oliver and I were feeling tired from our excesses the night before so headed back early.

Monday 6th August

I woke early and showered before the girls got ready, then we went to the café where we met Oliver and Fibbes. We arranged to meet them at the campsite at Cascais, west of Lisbon the following evening, so after carefully reversing the van out of the small space left by the idiots in the tent behind me, we set off for Lisbon. We didn't arrive until 4.30pm, and the temperature was high at 37 degrees and sticky. The girls needed to package up their rugs they had bought in Coimbra and send them back to Australia, so we spent nearly an hour in the post office boxing them up, a necessary but slow process. We arrived at the camp by 8.30pm and I spent the evening reading.

Tuesday 7th August

After breakfast I spent 30 minutes washing my clothes and hanging them out to dry. I went to the café for a drink and met two English guys who had been imprisoned overnight because one of them had headbutted a train guard! Myself and the girls then took the bus into Cascais centre to visit the shops and the market, but there's only so much shopping a guy can take so I left them in town and took the bus back, where the 'Boys from Cologne' arrived and I helped them put their tent up. The girls returned and we cooked food and drank eight bottles of wine between us, before Oliver and myself took a taxi into town (Fibbes was getting along famously with Wrongy so stayed behind). We were unable to get into the Coconut nightclub so we went to the John Bull pub, which was busy, and then onto a beach bar, which was very entertaining. We left with four bottles of wine and returned to camp, where we sat outside playing cards and drinking until 6am.

Wednesday 8th August

I still felt drunk in the morning when I woke up, no surprise there! Fibbes took the girls into Sintra while Ollie and myself got our heads in the right frame of mind and took a walk down to the beach and sunbathed. Later Fibbes and the girls met us and we sat around playing cards and drinking in a bar until 10pm. We then returned to camp and sat with three Kiwis playing a guitar and had a singalong until 2am. Fibbes slept with Wrongy in the tent while Ollie took a bunk in my van and the other girls slept outside.

Friday 10th August

Today was a bit of a marathon event. We all jumped in my van and headed to the market for the girls to buy more pottery, and afterwards I drove into Lisbon and parked on the quayside near the ferry terminal. We took the metal lift that takes you up to the old city level, part of which was still under construction after a huge fire had destroyed much of the town two years earlier. We spent the afternoon eating and drinking before I left them all and went into the castle as it was free entry. The inside had landscaped gardens with peacocks wandering around, and I was able to wander around the battlements taking in the view. Afterwards I met up with them all and we took a tram around the city before returning to the camp, dropping the girls off in Cascais on the way. We had arranged to meet them at 12 midnight at the John Bull pub, so Fibbes drove into town, and by chance we bumped into them earlier than arranged in another bar. Fibbes made a beeline for Wrongy, while Ollie and I sat at the bar ignoring them all. They had really started to get on my nerves, and meeting Ollie and Fibbes had evened the numbers up a bit and given me some male company. At 1am we all headed for Coconut disco, but we males could only enter with a female, so Ruth and Cait said they would wait by the entrance. However, when we arrived they were just going in with two French guys. Ollie and Fibbes managed to get in with Wrongy but this left me outside alone. After some persuasion from Fibbes, Cait came out to rescue me! We danced until 5am then decided to leave; however, as Ruth had disappeared, we stayed dancing until 5.45am when Ruth reappeared in tears. She had gone outside to look for us before re-entering. Fibbes drove back as dawn appeared over the horizon, and everyone went to bed except Ollie and me. We sat outside with another drink and had such a fit of the giggles that we started to wake up other campers at 7am!

Saturday 11th August

Cait woke us all up at 10am as she went to the toilets to be sick. Ollie was in one of my bunks, and as I looked outside I told Ollie that I could see strangers sitting at their table by their tent eating breakfast. It became apparent they were friends of Ollie and Fibbes called Martin and Eva, who were meeting up with them. Today we were leaving, so myself and the Aussie girls said our goodbyes. I promised to call into Cologne on my way back home and we left and headed eastwards towards Lisbon, across the suspension bridge which dominates the skyline, and then took the motorway south to Setubal, then towards Lagos. The girls had been sleeping for most of the journey so they felt refreshed when they woke but I felt tired from driving 170 miles, so when we hit Albufeira I told them I wasn't driving any further. It was 7pm when I stopped at the tourist office which happened to be closed; however, when I went to start the engine again it failed. I tried to bump start it but ended up double parked on the flat. The girls went for a walk while I looked at the engine. My patience with them was at breaking point – they were not including me in their conversations, not taking any notice of what I had to say or even replying to me. After asking three passing men to push the van, we got it started, but I then took the wrong turn and drove one and a half miles in the wrong direction. It was now dark and I couldn't find the campsite. I stopped for directions and after turning around eventually arrived at a big site. At reception we had to push the van again after I accidentally turned the engine off. After showering we decided an early night was in order, and things were getting frosty between us!

Sunday 12th August

After we bump started the van to leave, we headed towards Portimão and then Lagos. I didn't talk to the girls much at all on the journey. I also realised I needed a garage to check out the motor so asked in a tourist office in Lagos for a nearby VW garage but to no avail. The girls didn't seem to grasp the problem with the van and kept inquiring why I needed a garage. The girls went for a meal, and I informed them later that I was going to park on a hill overnight. They decided to rent a room for the night so I drove to the train station where we found various old ladies waiting for trains to arrive, where they encourage the passengers to rent their rooms. We picked one of the old ladies up and followed the direction of her pointed, shaking hand until we arrived at her house. We unloaded their baggage, and at last I felt free from them and their belongings. It was still early in the afternoon so we headed for the beach, but I didn't want to spend any more time in their company so I sat at a bar with a beer. When I returned 30 minutes later they had gone, so I walked up to a nearby hotel to find they were eating ice cream. They then told me they had hired a car for 10 days costing £72 each and that they were going to head back north to meet the guys from Cologne. I headed off to buy some groceries and on my return the girls were at the van, so we had a bottle of wine and then walked into town. I phoned Phil in England and felt that he couldn't wait to tell me that Sandy (my first wife if you had forgotten) was pregnant! Although we weren't together anymore it still felt a bit of a shock that she was expecting, especially as she had voiced opinions that she didn't want children. After some food and wine in a pizza restaurant I left the girls and slept in the van.

Monday 13ᵗʰ August

After nearly three weeks I was finally going to be free of the girls. I walked to their accommodation to check if they needed a lift and at 9.10am I picked them up and then dropped them off in town where I said my goodbyes. I headed back to Portimão and found a VW garage and spoke to the manager who put the van in the workshop to work on while I waited. He told me there was a loose connection which they had fixed, but I also had an oil leak so they needed to keep it overnight. This was not a problem as the manager agreed I could sleep in the van on the forecourt overnight. I then headed into town where I queued at the bank for 15 minutes to change a cheque, only to be told to go two doors down to an exchange office where I waited another 45 minutes, and then waited 15 minutes at the post office. After all that, I found a bar as I needed the toilet, and picked on Corkers Bar, run by Tony, where I sat and chatted to Tony, Jim, and his son Miles. Tony told me that the owner was happy for him to run the bar how he wanted to, if Tony 'wanted to change it to a gay bar, he could'. This didn't mean anything to me at the time. I needed a shower, so Tony suggested I use the one out the back which I accepted after a few beers. When I returned to the garage the manager had told me the work was finished, but that he was still happy for me to sleep on the forecourt. At 10pm I headed to Corkers where I met Tony again, but as the bar was quiet he closed it up and he, Paul and myself went to another bar to play pool with Stuart and Lucy. After Tony had left, Stuart and Lucy admitted that they thought Tony had picked me up as he was gay – this was a total surprise to me, my gaydar was broken!

After paying the garage for the work completed, I left Portimão and drove to Monte Gordo, the last town before entering Spain, where I camped overnight. The next day I took the ferry across the Guadiana River into Spain and headed for Seville, then on down to Marbella where I booked into the Buganvilla campsite for the evening.

Thursday 16th August

I left Marbella and headed for Fuengirola, and once I had a map of the town I headed for the nearest dentist as I had a filling that had fallen out and was giving me some pain. I was a bit apprehensive going to a Spanish dentist at first, I worried that it would not be as hygienic as it was in England. It would cost 6,000 pesetas, so I waited as they said they could do it straight away. I had an anaesthetic and it was all over in 20 minutes, and it was as good as it was at home. I lay on the beach for the afternoon before buying two chicken legs and vegetables for my evening meal. I then checked into the campsite and set up next to six French guys and one girl who were smoking cannabis and drinking wine. I cooked up too much food as usual and struggled to eat it all.

Friday 17th August

After six slices of toast for breakfast, I had decided to move on, so I went to take all my washing off the line when the guy at the line next to me spoke. He was from Bristol, his name was Simon and he was also on his own. After chatting to him for a while and we had got on well, I decided to stay longer. He was meeting his friends later that evening, so he jumped in the van and we spent the afternoon on the beach, where we spent most of our time laughing and eyeing up the local talent. After a few beers we returned to the camp, changed for the evening, and then walked back to town. We met his friends at the train station – they were all 17 years old – and we had a few drinks with them. Simon was being eyed up by an attractive girl, and after we egged him on he went over to talk to her and arranged to meet her at 2am at Club 27's. She was Swedish and her name was Jessica (must be a popular name in Sweden), and when she turned up at the club she looked stunning wearing a silver sequined dress. We got in for free and while Simon danced with Jessica I spent some time talking to her cousin who came with her; he was Finnish and very chatty. Simon's friends disappeared at 4.30am, so we then went to a club called Pinks which was right on the seafront. Again, we entered for free. Pinks' interior was decorated white and pink with a smoke machine spewing its contents across the room. We stayed until 6am, and when we exited the sun was rising over the horizon. As the beach beds were spread out in front of us we lay on them for 30 minutes before attempting the walk back. We arrived at the camp by 7.30am, where we had to jump the fence to get in as we had left our passes behind, then we hit the sack.

Saturday 18th August

After briefly waking at 9.30am, I went back to sleep until 2pm until it became unbearably hot. Simon needed some money but as the banks were closed I lent him 5,000 pesetas to tide him over. After lying on the beach until 7.45pm we returned to eat, and then changed ready to leave at 11.15pm, just the time I would be going home if I were on a night out in England. We walked to town and went to the London Bar where we met four girls. One was keen on Simon so we went to Roxy's club at 3.30am where Simon cracked on with her, and I sat and spoke to Michelle, Julia, Lucy and Steve. When I first met Julia I pretended I was French and using my best

English-speaking French accent (honed from watching 'Allo 'Allo) I strung her along for ages, while her friends Michelle and Steve also took part in the joke. At 5am we decided to go to Pinks but as we couldn't get in for free we returned to the camp. The girl that was keen on Simon slept in his tent.

Sunday 19th August

I woke by 12.30 lunchtime, had breakfast, and showered, and then Simon and I drove to Marbella to look for a place called Banana Beach, where apparently a band played live music all afternoon. After a drive around town and a beer in a pub called Franks Corner, we found it on the east side of town by the harbour. The place was thriving, the music was brilliant and people danced by the band, stood at the bar, or lay on sunbeds. We returned to the camp where we changed and then left by 8pm to find Nick and Rachel's apartment (Simon's friends). After some detective work we found them sitting on their patio. At 11pm we went to Lloyds Club, where by chance, I met Helen and Nicky, two girls I had previously spoken to about attending a timeshare meeting just to get the free alcohol they were giving away. Helen was from Nottingham working for seven weeks and would be finishing university the next year and planned to travel the world after that. We sat around until 1.30am, and as I felt ok to drive, we returned to town where I parked by the beach. Simon was feeling a bit drunk by now, but we persevered, had a Wimpy, and then went to Club 27's where the owner on the door questioned our free entry because we always quoted Jo's name (the girl who gave us free tickets the first time). He accused us of doing that every night (the cheek of it, but he was right of course!). When inside we were hassled by a waiter to buy a drink as we were just people-watching, so I suggested we leave separately which we did. Once at the van, because we were being watched by a group of lads, and we had decided to kip in the van, I drove to a building site where Simon slept on the floor between the two front seats.

Monday 20th August

We awoke by 9am and returned to the camp to clean ourselves up, before returning to town to get tickets for the timeshare deal. As expected Helen and Nicky didn't turn up, so we had an omelette sandwich in a café before lying on two beds on the beach until 4pm. We then returned to the café to have another omelette sandwich! After returning the van to the camp, we walked down town to a busy bar, where I spent time eyeing up two attractive girls who I reckoned were Swedish. All of a sudden Jessica appeared and stood between us talking to Simon. Everyone fancied Simon, tall with blond hair and a chiselled jaw – who could blame them! We left to go to the London Pub, and on the way we spoke to two more Swedish girls, Ulrika and (believe it or not) another Jessica, so they joined us for a drink and we used their lipstick to draw the Underground Club pass on our arms. They stamp it on your arm to prove you've paid, which worked and we entered for free. We had a few dances. I fancied Ulrika, but Simon kept jumping in and talking to her. The girls eventually left so we sat outside at 4am having food for an hour. We arrived at the camp by 7.30am, and although I hadn't been successful this evening, Simon had been blown out four times, which made me feel better!

Wednesday 22nd August/Thursday 23rd August/Friday 24th August

We went out late on the Tuesday evening and at 1am we arrived at Roxys for a few drinks. Simon took a photo for three girls from Liverpool, Julie, Julia, and Stephanie. We then all decided to go on to Pinks and dance the night away, not leaving until 8am. Afterwards we walked with the girls to their apartment at Ronda 3 where they were staying. On the way there we bought some beer from a vending machine and were given some marijuana by a random stranger. We sat on their balcony eating food, drinking beer, and smoking a joint and all got a bit silly and started to throw food at passing pedestrians from the 8th floor. We slept from 11am until 5pm, then we went to the beach for a few hours before Simon and I returned to the camp and changed. We then returned to Ronda 3 where we sat drinking tequila until 1am, then went into town and spent the night at 27's before returning to Ronda 3 at 6.30am where I slept until 11am. The afternoon was spent at the swimming pool playing games and drinking before Simon and I returned to camp for a nap. I quite liked Stephanie but decided to play 'hard to get' by telling them that we were not going to meet them this evening. However, we bumped into them at Roxy's and then ended up at Pinks until 8.30am. Stephanie was all over me – obviously playing 'hard to get' does work! As Simon had pulled a Spanish girl called Annabella, I took a taxi back to Ronda 3 with the girls where we set an alarm for 11am as the girls were going home that morning. Unfortunately, no-one heard the alarm, and it wasn't until the tour rep came dashing into their room that everyone woke up. After a mad dash to pack everything in 20 minutes they unfortunately missed their coach to the airport, so I gave them 1000 pesetas to take a taxi, and we said our goodbyes. When I returned to camp Simon was just going to the beach so I decided to sleep by the pool all day and then walk into town to meet Simon where we had a meal. It had been a hectic three days non-stop partying, and although I tried to extend it a bit longer that evening, I gave up and returned to camp at 3am.

Sunday 26ᵗʰ August

I had returned to the camp at 9.30am after a hectic Saturday night out and about, and as I had decided to check out of the site, I paid 17,500 pesetas for the 10 nights. Simon was in his tent asleep and I wasn't able to wake him, so I drove down to town and parked near Pinks and went to sleep in the van. Simon later came to town and woke me at 1pm and we took two beds on the beach where we slept until 6pm. Simon had decided to go back to pack his tent up, so I dropped him off in town to get some cash, but as he seemed to have disappeared and I couldn't find him I re-parked the van. I got changed and then bumped into Julia and Lucy and we went to the London Underground as entry was free before midnight. I then met Ulrika and Jessica and I was feeling great that I had these four good looking girls all to myself. We stayed there until 2.30am but I then had to return to my van to get my cash card. On approaching it, I wondered who had dumped a load of rubbish by my van, but on closer inspection I realised it was Simon asleep in his sleeping bag on a wooden beach bed he had dragged across the road, with his tent dumped beside him. Well, I just couldn't stop laughing at such a sight! Simon went to sleep in the van while I went out until 4.30am.

Monday 27th August

On awakening, we left town and headed to Torremolinos and parked up at the beach. I got a map from the tourist office, and we familiarised ourselves with the town, before having a quiet night out, just drinking cola.

After the excesses of the previous week, we had a very quiet Tuesday and Wednesday, spending time on the beach talking to groups of Spanish girls, and having our laundry washed in the launderette.

Saturday 1st September

We didn't wake until noon, after which we went to a local café for a coffee. I returned before Simon, and as I approached the van I noticed the side door was open. On inspection I noticed that our jeans had gone, and Simon's rucksack and bag had gone. We had noticed a suspicious looking couple in a Citroen car parking next to us when we left, but didn't think too much about it. We then went to the police station for Simon to make a report before he rang Visa to report a stolen card, a job he had his father eventually do, and to report a stolen passport. Simon had to wear my shorts and T-shirt out for the evening, which was spent drinking at El Open Arms, Garfields, Jax, Splash and Venya's where I bumped into Sylvia, a girl I had met a few evenings before.

Monday 3rd September

This morning we packed up and drove to Malaga to visit the British consulate, which we arrived at just as it opened. Simon needed to get a new passport issued and arrange for his dad to book a flight from Malaga, the tickets he would pick up at the airport. We went to the shops to pass the time before driving to the port area where I parked for the night, and we had food. About 3am I needed a wee so went outside for one, and on my return, because it was so hot, I only pulled the side door to an almost closed position and went back to sleep.

Tuesday 4th September

When I awoke, I noticed the side door was fully open, so I asked Simon if he had been outside, to which he replied "No". I then started laughing as I noticed his washbag, virtually the only thing he still owned, had gone missing from on top of the cooker. Then, on looking for my wallet, I noticed my Toblerone bag was missing, which contained my diary, Filofax and all the addresses I had collected. I wasn't concerned for my wallet, but more for my personal belongings. It was still dark outside, but I decided to take a look around, and in the flowerbed less than 20 feet away I found everything except my money. What a relief! My bag was positioned up next to my head while I was sleeping, so they would have had to stretch over me to reach it, which was a very frightening prospect. After collecting our thoughts, we headed for the police station (again) to make a report. There was a small queue, but as it was only 9.15am, we weren't too concerned. However, as criminals were brought in they jumped the queue, along with others who had appointments. After some complaining that we had to be at the airport by 1pm, we were eventually seen at 12.30pm. On returning to the van, I had collected a parking ticket. I didn't have any cash to pay for one when we arrived as it had all been stolen, but I wasn't intending to pay the fine anyway. After a dash to the airport, and a quick coffee, I said goodbye to Simon at 2pm, him wearing my shorts, my T-shirt and owing me £55. I left Malaga and drove nonstop for six hours, wanting to put some distance between myself and that dreadful place! I stopped at a campsite in Totana, 248 miles away, where I went to sleep, doors locked!

A letter I received from Simon later.

Martin, are you back? Well, when you read this you will be, so you'll know what it's like to have all the luxuries back. Just the little things like washing, sleeping, and eating. Nobody recognised me at home due to the aging effect you had on me.

I got stopped at passport control as they didn't believe the British consulate would give me a pass with no ID. Eventually he let me through after ringing my father. Next was customs. I couldn't help laughing, walking to about 5 guards with my sleeping bag wrapped around what appeared to be a bomb. You and I know it was a tent but they got suspicious when the first question they asked was 'can I see your passport sir?' to which I replied 'No, I haven't got one'. You see, passport control had kept hold of the emergency one. Next was the coach home. One of the guards told me there was a charity office in Heathrow which would pay for your ticket home but when I got there they would only give me £2 towards the £18 required. It all worked out ok in the end as my father paid for the ticket at his end. I know you thought I had given you a false address so I could keep the 'trendy' shorts but I'm afraid you will have to have them back so you can look silly wearing them. No, seriously thanks for the loan and the clothes. I just couldn't handle travelling home in my trunks and flip flops! Where else did you travel or did you leave pleasant Malaga and head for home. When you do arrive home we'll have to meet up and talk about our wild times. It's just started to rain so I'm going to run around naked in the back garden!!

Thanks for the help. Hans (Simon)

Wednesday 5th September

Today was another travelling day, I left the site at 9.30am and apart from three stops during the day, I passed Murcia, Alicante, Valencia, and Tarragona before checking in at a site just past Sitges called Albatross, 11 hours later, having covered 403 miles in total.

Thursday 6th September

I managed to have a hot shower, only my second one in three weeks, before driving into Barcelona to have a look around the shops where I bought a few records. Early afternoon I left town heading north until I reached a small town called Figueras, where I had to stop and send a postcard to singlet Ian, who has the same surname. After I crossed the border into France I headed to Canet-Plage near Perpignan to a campsite.

Friday 7th September

I awoke to a pretty windy day. I had another hot shower and set off towards Sete, where I purchased oranges, grapes, and peaches to put some goodness back into my body. I had a bad cold and felt run-down and tired, not surprising after my recent excesses. I stopped in Arles and had a look around; it is such a beautiful city, twinned with York, well worth visiting. Having missed signs to a site west of Marseilles I took the port road into town, again, a beautiful sight of the port and town as you descend the hill, where I booked into the municipal campsite on the east side of town.

Saturday 8th September

I spent the morning shopping in town buying some CDs to listen to before I headed for Toulon. Just past there is a beach called Salins Plage, which happened to be a nudist beach swarming with naked men 'standing up and looking around'. I wonder if they would do that if they had trunks on? After a couple of hours reading at the far end of the beach, I checked into a campsite.

Sunday 9th September

My cold was improving and I started to enjoy the sunshine again. I was gradually in RAS (Recovery After Simon!) and getting my strength back. After topping up my tan in the morning I headed off towards St Tropez, which was about 20 miles away. I had read or heard something on the news about forest fires in southern France and saw that mile after mile as far as you could see, every tree or bush was burnt. The hills were dead and blackened although the vineyards, being relatively low lying escaped with minor burns at the edges. After spending the afternoon in St Tropez looking around the shops I booked into the 'Prairie of the Sea' site costing 76 Francs for the night. After eating I went to the bar to find on a large screen Ghostbusters 2 was being shown followed by Twins, both films I had seen before but I enjoyed the evening doing nothing but lounging around, something I hadn't done for months.

Tuesday 11th September

Having moved the few miles along the coast to Antibes where I now found myself, I took in Nice town followed by a drive to Monte Carlo, where I had a walk around the shops, saw the casino and the harbour with all the expensive boats moored up. Then I rang up David, an

Italian who lived in Turin who came to work in England on a work exchange at Sandy's place of work; he had lodged with us for the duration. I arranged to meet him the following evening at the campsite I had planned to stay at. That evening I spent with an English couple called Paul and Jo from Farnborough, who had camped next to me in their van. They were headed for Greece but had been in Jersey for six months where they had got married.

Wednesday 12th September

After saying goodbye to my neighbours, I set off for Menton where, on the spur of the moment I decided to have one last swim in the sea, which was very refreshing considering I still felt drunk after we had drank a bottle of Zoco the night before. I had a very scenic drive north up the mountain towards the French Italian border, through a two-mile-long tunnel which took you into Italy and on towards Turin. After a wrong turn and sitting in rush-hour traffic, and asking five different people where the campsite was, I arrived to find it had closed down. I quickly found another option, booked in, changed, and then returned to the closed site where I sat at the gates for one hour waiting for David, who didn't turn up.

Thursday 13th September

After breakfast I wandered into Turin to look around. The city is extremely beautiful, large square buildings standing guard over numerous small shops, set under arches nestled away from the road, protecting them from the sun. I bought a few clothes, a T-shirt and sweatshirt, then spent the afternoon lying by the edge of the river Po, passing time until I returned to the camp to eat and have an early night.

Saturday 15th September

After three days in Turin, and no success getting back in contact with David, I decided to move on. Yesterday I had taken out 200,000 lira, spent 79,000 lira on a pair of jeans (£36) and put 45,000 lira of fuel into the van. I then realised I would need more cash for the weekend but as the banks were closed I would need to find another cashpoint. At Novara west of Milan I took out another 200,000 lira and in a shop asked directions for the road to Stresa, at which point a woman customer said, 'follow me' in Italian hand signs. As she jumped into her car and sped off I hastily ran to the van and chased her. She sped down the road through red lights and cut up other cars, I had to do the same thing just to keep up, narrowly avoiding an accident. It was a bit like a car chase scene, but eventually she stopped and directed me straight on, then disappeared. I had earlier noticed a problem with the driver's side wing mirror and on inspection it fell off in my hand due to a broken screw. Realising it was unrepairable until England, I sellotaped it up as best as I could, albeit with limited viewing. I continued north to Stresa and along the banks of Lake Maggiore and on to Bellinzona where I then headed up the Alps to the St Gotthard pass, 15 kilometres up hairpin bends up to cloud level. After exiting the tunnel to begin the 19-kilometre descent, the rain came down heavily, the first I had seen for three months, and I switched on the heater in the van to keep warm. I stopped at a camp at Altdorf. I was now in Switzerland and was a bit surprised to hear German being spoken as I had not intended to return north in this direction. I had a meal in the restaurant of salad and veal in breadcrumbs with chips, a total surprise as I had no idea what I was ordering.

Sunday 16th September

In the morning it was cloudy and cold when I headed towards Zurich on the motorway but decided to call in at Zurich airport to buy a newspaper. I swept into the car park with 0.1 metre height to spare under the barrier, ran into the terminal and returned to the van in no time at all. I then took the road to Bulach unaware I would be crossing into Germany as a checkpoint loomed up.

"Have you anything to declare?" he asked.

"No," I replied.

"Park over there–" he pointed as he walked off with my passport to check it. This was the first border I had crossed where anyone had looked at my photo, but he soon returned and waved me off. Further down the road as I crossed back into Switzerland I had the same treatment, before re-entering Germany again and heading through the Schwarzwald forest and on to Freiburg. After frequently crossing borders I decided not to visit Strasbourg as soon as I realised it was across the border in France.

Monday 17th September

What a cold night last night! I slept with my clothes on, in a sleeping bag, under a blanket and under my thick Portuguese rug but I was still cold. After breakfast and a hot shower, I tried the engine but it wouldn't start; the battery seemed flat. After changing the two batteries around to no avail, I asked a French couple if they had any jump leads. They directed me to a group of Germans, and after some crude drawings I had already prepared, I got the message across and they drove their car over followed by six friends to watch the proceedings. It worked and I left for Achem where I found a VW garage just closing for lunch, so I hung around until opening time where they took 20 minutes to put a new battery in. I continued my journey to Heidelberg where I had a look around town, buying a CD and a shirt. I also went into a chemist and asked the pharmacist.

"Could I buy a Ventolin inhaler please."

"They are a prescription item," he replied.

"My doctor told me it was possible to buy them over the counter in Europe," I said.

"Where are you from?" he asked.

"England," I replied.

"Well England IS in Europe," he stated. "I thought you were from further afield."

He had a point! He relented and sold me one for 35 Deutschmarks. I rang Fibbes in Koln to arrange my visit.

Tuesday 18th September

I headed north to Frankfurt before going to Budingen, a small town where a German guy called Joe lived. He had also lodged with Sandy and I on a work exchange trip to Alton some years before, and I decided to see if I could find him. As I entered the town I called into the police station where I got directions and drove straight to the address. On inspection of the name tags on the door I discovered that his name appeared so I pressed the buzzer. He was shocked to see me – after all I had given no warning. We walked down into town where he showed me the old town before visiting a bar where we sat and drank until 1am. We returned to Joe's apartment, perched high up on the hillside overlooking Budingen, where, after a nightcap I slept on the couch.

Thursday 20th September

Last night I had phoned Fibbes and we arranged to meet in the morning near his home, even though Fibbes was flying to London in the afternoon to visit Wrongy (the Aussie). After a slight panic when the engine failed to start again, I bumped it and set off for Rodenskirchen, a suburb of Cologne, where I met Fibbes. He took me to his family home, a grand apartment overlooking the Rhine, a very exclusive and very expensive area, where I met his mother and brother Oliver. Fibbes' brother Oliver and I took Fibbes to the airport as his flight was at 5pm, then after returning I waited for Ollie (Kuepper, from my time in Portugal) to finish work and pick me up. We then went back to his mother's house where I met his brothers Klaus and Frank, a lovely family. At 9pm we went to a music studio where their group Die La Tents met to discuss future songs (they had won a music competition while in Portugal and had to fly back home to perform). At 11.30pm Ollie and I left to go to a bar and then onto a club called 42's before returning at 4.30am.

Friday 21st September

I awoke in Fibbes' flat at 10am where I met a Norwegian guy called Eskil, who had another room there. Ollie arrived by 2pm, having taken the day off work, and we went into the town centre, had a few beers in a bar, then ascended Cologne cathedral to the top for a fantastic view of the city. After a chicken burger and chips meal we returned to Ollie's mum's house where she cooked spaghetti bolognaise which I couldn't eat, and then returned to the town where we all met up again and visited various bars. This was a very heavy session of drinking finalised by Martin, Eva and myself attending a bar called Pink Champagne until 6.30am.

Saturday 22nd September

Ollie picked me up at 12 noon to have breakfast at his house, before picking up Andy and Eva and going to the horse-racing track in the north of the city. We put money into a pool and picked two horses per race with a little success. We returned to Cologne, had pork and sauerkraut for dinner, a short nap, and were picked up at 10pm when we went to Eva's flat where we played cards. I showed them how to play the card game that singlet Ian had taught me on the beach at San Sebastian. At midnight we headed for the bars where we drank until

3am. We then visited a large hall in an industrial area where there was a massive party taking place. We stayed until early morning then we took a taxi back at 6.30am.

Sunday 23rd September

I didn't wake until 1.30pm and waited until Ollie collected me at 4pm. We were both incredibly tired, and as I hadn't eaten we went to a McDonald's for food before heading to the fair. I didn't want to drink today but after meeting Andy and Eva I had about seven beers which gave me a buzz again. The beer on sale in Cologne is unique to the city; called Kolsch it is served in a 0.2 Lt Stange glass, a type of tumbler which is so paper thin you could crush it with your hand. When ordering from the waiters, they bring all the beers on a tray to your table and then mark a beermat with marks corresponding to the number of beers, adding marks for every additional order. When you leave, they total up the beers on the beermat and the bill is split between the group. Later we went to Karlsbad where we stayed until 12.30am.

Monday 24th September

I awoke by 10am, and Eskil drove me to my van which was parked in the yard of Fibbes' family. There I met

Oliver (brother to Fibbes) who said he would accompany me for the day to the museums. After a coffee, we went to his works at the radio station where he sometimes reads the news, then headed for the museums which were unfortunately closed. I then returned to my van and drove to Ollie's mum's house where I gave her a bouquet of flowers as a thank you for feeding me regularly. After dinner Ollie, Klaus and myself went to the fair until 10pm then on to Karlsbad again where we drank until 3am.

Tuesday 25th September

Time to head home! After taking a taxi to Rodenskirchen to drop off the keys to the flat and say my goodbyes, I took the motorway towards Aachen, into Belgium and onwards past Brussels to the ferry terminal at Oostende. I queued for the 5.45pm ferry, where coincidentally parked in front of me was the light blue VW camper van containing the four Kiwis I had first met in Biarritz and then San Sebastian. I eventually arrived in Dover at 9pm, then took the motorway back to Alton where I arrived at Mum's by 11.50pm and knocked on the door to surprise Mum and Bill. This was the end of a very exciting, exhausting, hot, friendly, and eventful period of my life, one that I will always remember.

ME? INTERESTING?

On returning to Alton, I lived with Mum and Bill in Beechwood Road, but my immediate thought was to get in contact with my 'singlet' mates, so I turned up at 'singlet' Andy's house hoping he was back from work, only to find his now girlfriend Annette and her friend Dee at the house. After introducing myself 'la bise' style, the French greeting kiss on both cheeks, definitely never experienced in sleepy old Alton, we chatted until Andy was due back, whereupon I hid in his cupboard, jumping out on his arrival to surprise him. We had a good catch up and arranged our next night out. It turns out that Dee had previously been a girlfriend of singlet Phil and singlet Ian, and as singlet Andy was in a relationship, I started dating her.

This became very complicated following my visit to a married friend's house for drinks and to enthral them with my stories from my trip. The evening was arranged and I duly arrived. We sat in the lounge drinking and chatting, the evening flowed perfectly, the drink flowed easily, and as the night wore on I was offered to stay over instead of driving home. My friends decided to go to bed, and as they did I noticed someone sat in the corner of the room, someone I don't remember seeing before, someone who I swear hadn't spoken all night. It was the wife's sister. I was taken aback; I know it doesn't seem possible but I really felt that it happened this way. My friends went to bed and I sat talking to her. We got along very well, so well that we had sex right there on the lounge floor! The walls and ceiling weren't very thick and it became apparent to the wife upstairs what was going on. I started to see this woman more regularly, as well as seeing Dee, which was a dangerous game to play, but exciting along with it. On one occasion I was in Alton with this woman when I spied Dee, who by now knew we were over, coming towards us. I had to play a game of cat and mouse, diving into shops in one door and out through another door, rushing around trying to lose her which I eventually did. Later that evening at Mum's we had the house to ourselves, when the telephone rang and on answering it I had a lot of abuse directed towards me from Dee. Eventually I hung up and lied that it was a wrong number. The wife's sister eventually rented a house of her own and I helped her move in, except that there was a connection with Sandy, my ex-wife, who was happy to lend her a bed and washing machine. I went to Sandy's dad's outbuildings and picked them up for her and moved them in. The issue was, and I never mentioned it, was that this was mine and Sandy's double bed from our time together. I ended up sleeping in my own bed! There was another major issue that was difficult to deal with. As a result of our first night together, the wife's sister became pregnant! She was adamant she would have a termination, a decision that was out of my hands. I accompanied her to the appointment and recall driving back in silence. We broke up soon after, it was never a serious relationship on my behalf and I knew we were not going to be together, she wasn't my type.

The stories from my travels had a profound effect on girls. An evening in my company with me recounting my experiences and tales, and they seemed to fall at my feet. Never before had I been so interesting, and girls were intrigued. This applied to Caroline, who was the younger sister of one of my college acquaintances, and very attractive. After an evening together, we started seeing each other. She lived in London, her parents lived in Holybourne. She was quite sporty and liked running, even entering marathons. We had a while together, but it all seemed to fall apart one evening when I was invited to the theatre in London with her family. They made me feel substandard, that I was not good enough for her, and I really felt awkward. She was certainly posher than I was. One evening after staying with her at her parents' house while they were away, we had an argument and I decided to walk home. She came after me in her car and eventually turned up at my mum's house where we decided to call it a day. Sometime later in the new year I bumped into her in town where she tried to tell me about her failure in the London marathon, but I never gave her the chance to speak and walked away, ignoring her. That evening after returning home, the doorbell went and she walked into the kitchen where I totally ripped into her and her previous attitude towards me. She ran out of the house in tears, and in hindsight, I felt really awful for treating her that way. I'd never been so harsh on anyone like that before, especially a female. I hope she's having a wonderful life.

DANA

In March of 1991 singlet Ian and I had been making trips to Basingstoke hospital on a Thursday evening because it was disco night in the Breakaway, a club situated on the hospital premises. Ian knew a friend who was in training as a nurse, and disco night meant nurses! This particular night we were with Ian's friend Sonya and a few of her friends when I decided to ask one of them if they wanted to dance. However, the girl I asked had a boyfriend and knowing this fact, another nurse called Dana quickly stepped in and said, "I will". It was a slow dance and as Dana and I held each other, we looked across to see Ian and Sonya dancing and burst out laughing. Ian was bent over attempting to kiss Sonya – she was at least 10 inches shorter than him and the whole image just set us off, we were unable to stop. At the end of the evening, we all agreed we should go out together as a foursome, for a few drinks. Dana was a cute girl, she was 5 foot 4 inches tall, she had long curly dark hair, a gorgeous cheeky smile, and a northern accent. The following week we all met up and had a drink in a local pub. I found out that she was 19 years old from a place called Boldon Colliery near South Shields, way up in the north east, where she lived with her mum Kathleen and stepdad Ken. She also had two sisters, Claire and Phillipa. She was studying to be a nurse on a scheme called Project 2000, which was to contract the training of nurses out to British universities. Nurses studied for three years, splitting the time between class-based learning and practical placements. She had a small room with a bed in the nurses' accommodation building, which had access to a shared kitchen and bathrooms. I visited Dana's room on a number of occasions and I should have taken note of the tidiness, or untidiness, of the room. The floor could not be seen below the clothes and items scattered around, so maybe she blinded me by her beauty! She had a vulnerability about her and used to put makeup on which almost painted her face white, with a thin curly strand of hair falling down over her eyes and face, almost as if she wanted to hide. When we started dating I used to tell her that she didn't need the makeup plastered on so heavily, and being 12 years older, I felt she needed looking after. Maybe it was my paternal feelings coming through, maybe they were feelings of something stronger. We started seeing each other when we could and our first date alone was at a stock car racing night at Tongham near Aldershot. My elder brother Brian used to take me with him when I was younger, and I loved the sight of the superstock cars racing around the track, the banger cars smashing into each other, and the destruction derby which was a 'last car moving' event. The smell of oil and petrol, the dark night and the floodlights lighting up the arena made a lasting impression on me. We dated throughout the year, taking trips to the Isle of Wight with singlet Phil and his girlfriend Julie, who was pregnant at the time, and Dana came with me to Cologne in December '91 on a coach trip to visit the Christmas market. It was purely a cheap way to get to Cologne because when we did, we spent the entire weekend with the friends I had made on my travels. When we saw Eva and Martin again they asked me what the name of the game of cards was that I taught them on my travels, to which I replied, "I don't know". They then told me that they had named it after me,' Birdie', and had taught it to all their friends. I am amused to think that in Cologne the game of Birdie is widely played by many people and is spreading throughout the city. All my family and friends who play the game also call it Birdie! On the morning of our return trip, we only got back to the hotel about two hours before we had to leave, still drunk from staying up all night. We had also bought a few chocolate items at the Christmas market, and we safely stored them under our coach seat only to find out later that the heater below had melted them all.

On the employment front I didn't seek work of any kind until February of '91 when, through an acquaintance, I started working for a company called Gazelle Couriers, based in Basingstoke. I travelled all over the UK delivering parcels, even making one trip overnight to Paris in a Ford Transit van. I crossed the Channel by ferry from Portsmouth and had a bunk in a small cabin with four beds in; privacy was provided by a curtain drawn across the front. This job was purely for pin money to give me something to spend without dipping anymore into my bank account and the money I had left from the sale of my last house. With that in mind I decided I needed to get back into full time work and using the saying 'it's not what you know but who you know' I decided to ring up my old boss from Suchard to have a chat with him. I found out that he had left Suchard and was now working for a sweet manufacturer called Swizzels Matlow who were based near Manchester. He described how the size of the orders were phenomenal compared to the last job, and that they were looking for someone to work in London and the south. On that basis I applied for a position and was accepted, and on 20th May 1991 I became a salesman for Swizzels. Selling had become the only trade I knew about; even if I wanted a career change, what could I do? I had no qualifications other than a good basic training in sales.

Soon after, in July I moved out of Mum's house into my newly purchased house for £60,000 at 35 Haydock Close, yes, the same Haydock Close I lived in with

Sandy, but now I had gone from the detached number 1 to the end of terraced number 35. It had 2 bedrooms, a living room attached to a small kitchen with an archway between the rooms giving it a bright feel. There was also a small garden out the back, and out the front it had a tiny patch of grass before a pathway leading to communal parking spaces.

Dana and I were now a regular item. She was still training in Basingstoke but she would stay with me on her weekends off. We socialised regularly with my singlet friends and their partners, Phil and Julie, Andy and Anette, and Ian, who liked to flit from one girl to another rather than getting bogged down in an ongoing relationship. We had our first holiday abroad in August '92 to Sunny Beach Bulgaria, where the lasting memory is of a hotel room which had silverfish crawling around the bathroom and on the walls of the bedroom where we slept. Bulgaria was cheap, a pint of beer was 28p and a meal out was a few pounds. One evening we attended a beach party, and one of the competitions Dana and I volunteered for. They were looking for three couples to swop clothes as fast as possible, done under a large canvas sack big enough for two people. How hard could it be? After all, we were hidden. Each couple were covered over and the task began, Dana put on my t-shirt and shorts while I was in the process of putting on her clothes, when all of a sudden, the canvas was whipped off and I am stood there naked in front of an audience of 200 people. I quickly grabbed my bollocks and ran down the beach away from the crowd. I found out later that their intention was always to whip off the canvas regardless of progress.

Our relationship had grown stronger so in October I contacted Sandy and asked if she could fill in the forms so that we could get divorced, which she agreed to (it was such an amicable split). The divorce was finalised in February 1993. Sometime in May when Dana and I were lying in bed I asked her a question:

"Would you like to move in with me?"

"No, because my mum would kill me," she replied.

"Well, what would make you move in?"

"A ring on my finger," she said.

So, I replied, "Hypothetically, would you move in if we got married?"

"Of course, I would," she said laughing.

Gosh, I was such a romantic. After my hypothetical proposal we set about arranging a wedding and, because Dana had holiday dates already booked for September, we chose Saturday 4th September, to be held in Boldon where she was from, in the north east. There was a sense of similarity between mine and Dana's plans together, and my marriage to Sandy, where a decision to marry in May resulted in a wedding in September. In the future this did result in confusion for me as to which date was my anniversary with Dana! When I started dating Dana, her mother Kathleen was not happy with the fact that

I was 12 years older, but the fact I was divorced as well made it even worse. Having said that, whenever I met her mum we got on like a house on fire; it was either because we were both Capricorns or because I had such a charming personality! Dana was a Catholic so for her to marry a divorcee meant it would be impossible for us to marry in a Catholic church, so she set about finding an alternative venue, which came in the name of the Boldon United Reformed Church. She arranged flowers, transport, a wedding dress, and bridesmaids' dresses, plus a reception which was to be held at a Catholic club in Jarrow, followed by an evening disco upstairs at The Marine pub at the end of Ocean Drive in South Shields. All this was achieved while living in Alton and the occasional trip back to the north east.

Two days before the wedding Dana found out that she was pregnant. She was at Julie's house and mentioned that she felt sick, and as Julie had a spare pregnancy test, she used it. It came back positive. This came as a massive surprise to Dana because when she was 18 and had been suffering from bad pain, she had seen a specialist who told her that she had polycystic ovaries and would be unlikely to have children without fertility treatment. Obviously the specialist had not met Mr Super Sperm! I also had a dilemma – who do I choose as a best man, singlet Phil, Andy, or Ian? In the end I made an unusual decision, I had all three of them as best men. Come the day, the wedding went smoothly, attended by all Dana's relatives plus everyone that had to journey from the south. At the time of the speeches my best men decided to retire me from the Singlet club as I was now married, by presenting me with the homemade medal that we used to pass around to the Singlet who pulled the ugliest woman. Wait, are they insinuating I had married the ugliest woman? We spent our wedding night at the Sir William Fox Hotel in Westoe village, famous as the birthplace of Sir William Fox, three-times prime minister of New Zealand. We then went on to the Lake District where we stayed four nights at The Ghyll Head Hotel at Waterhead, the room with a four-poster bed costing £27.50 per night.

On 20th May 1994 Dana was induced and at 11.04pm she gave birth to a baby girl who weighed nine pounds and three ounces. When she was born, at first, she wouldn't breathe and the midwives seemed a little panicked. It was a few minutes before they got her breathing. As soon as she was ok, she was handed to me, and I cradled her and sang to her Prince's song 'The most beautiful girl in the world' which was number one in the pop charts that week. I had tears in my eyes as I sang. This was such an amazing experience, the best day in my life seeing my daughter born, I couldn't ask for anything more and I was so proud of Dana. She did a wonderful job despite me squeezing water in her eyes like a waterfall, instead of mopping her brow! We named her Emily Claire. Now the job of parenting begins, two adults with no idea what they have to do with this tiny baby in the hands of beginners. We had a cot assembled in our bedroom so we could keep an eye on her. Dana breastfed Emily initially, and during the night when she cried I would get her from the cot and pass her to Dana to feed while she was lying in bed, half asleep. Over time Emily went onto bottles, and I would get up in the night and heat up the bottle, which was full of expressed breast milk, and feed her. I don't know how we coped over those weeks, it all seemed to blur into one. Eventually we put Emily in the spare room because after five weeks she had started to sleep through the night. We had a baby monitor in her room so we could hear her cry when we were downstairs. However, we agreed that we wouldn't make a rod for our own backs by mollycoddling her, and in due course, when we heard her crying we let her cry. To save interrupting us downstairs we even turned the volume on the monitor off so we could only see the green lights change into red lights when the noise got loud. Were we bad parents? We had seen the results of bad parenting first hand from friends and we didn't want to go down the same path. In the long run it seemed to work as she learnt that she wouldn't get picked up because she cried and bedtimes improved. Emily liked to have a dummy which, I must admit, I encouraged because it gave me some peace, but Dana argued against it. On one particular holiday in the Lake District when Emily was two years old,

Dana and Emily's granny kept taking the dummy from her to break the habit she was relying on, while I kept pulling dummies out of every pocket I had and sticking them in her mouth. It was a comical situation, dummies concealed all about myself! Just six months later, Dana was pregnant again, which was great news. We had gone from 'probably' not being able to have children due to Dana's polycystic ovaries, to expecting a second child in no time at all. On 30th August 1995 Dana was induced again and gave birth to another girl who weighed in at eight pounds 13 ounces whom we named Lauren Louise. While Dana was in hospital having Lauren, Mum came to stay with me to help look after Emily. I had a long black towelling dressing gown which over time had split down the seam on my right-hand side. One morning after picking Emily up from her cot, with Mum standing next to me, I had a feeling that the split side was in an embarrassing position, so without looking down, I pulled the gown across my body to the left side, which left the split framing my genitals to my mum. She looked down and said, "God, no wonder Dana gets pregnant". How embarrassing! Sometime before Lauren was born I had seen an old film featuring Lauren Bacall and I was mesmerised by her beauty, so I wanted the name Lauren. Louise was after my grandmother who had the same middle name. I had also seen the old black and white film version of Little Women on TV and was determined that I wanted four girls for children; by chance Dana also wanted four girls. Before our two girls were born we discussed names for boys and girls, not knowing whether we were going to have a boy or girl. Dana liked the name Matthew, and as my footballing hero was Matt Le Tissier, I would only agree on the name Matthew if one of the middle names was Le Tissier. However, as they were girls it didn't happen, but I still regret not giving the name Le Tissier to at least one of my girls – that would be a conversation piece for the future. As a keepsake for both my girls, the day following both their births I bought every newspaper printed as they contained the news from the day they were born, with the idea to present to them on their 18th birthdays, which I did.

With Dana's impending second birth I put the house up for sale in the July knowing that living in Haydock Close in a small two-bedroom terraced house with two small children would be a bit of a squeeze. Since I had bought the house the market had been in the doldrums, so I could only put the house up for sale at the same price I had paid. In the meantime, we found a lovely property in Rookswood on the other side of town and by the end of November we had completed the sale and purchased number 26 for £75,500. We moved in seamlessly, the house was a three-bedroomed property, with a garage fronting the house, behind which was an entrance porch and hall. The kitchen was to the right, then through a passageway to the right of the stairs was a decent sized lounge with French doors into the garden. It had a front and rear garden, which would be great for the girls to play in. Emily's development was significant. I used to walk her around the road naming the colours of each garage door, which she learnt quickly, and could soon identify the colours herself. She even started taking responsibility for Lauren, a younger sister to look after. She was keen to assist at every opportunity, feeding her, handing her toys, even talking gobbledygook baby talk to her. We installed new double glazing, paid for with free shares from Sun Life Financial of Canada who went public after we had taken out a policy, which was a good decision by Dana at the time.

On the work front, things were going well for me at Swizzels. I had found a sales position which for once I was enjoying, it was such a friendly company to work for, and I have since said it was the most enjoyable sales job I had ever had. Testament to the fact that the company was very good to work for was backed up by the long service current colleagues had given to the company, 20…30…35 years' employment.

I was in my fourth year when I had a visit from Ken, who was the National Sales manager, for a day's work in London. He had come down to see me to find out my thoughts and ambitions as regards possible promotion in the future. I think I made it pretty clear what sort of management material I would be when we had lunch in a greasy spoon café. We had both ordered sausage, egg and chips when I picked up the sugar dispenser and poured it all over my food thinking it was salt! Not a good move in hindsight. In actual fact I told him that I was happy in my current situation, the number one priority in my life was my wife and children. I felt that if I was to take promotion in the future I would be spending time away from them, something I wasn't prepared to do. In my heart, I wanted to be there for them, something that my father was not able to do for me. My family completed me, I had a purpose in life, to look after, to provide for, to care for, to be there for them all. Nothing else mattered in life, they were my life now, and I loved my children so much, I would sacrifice my own life for them. Before we had Lauren, Dana had started working at Winchester hospital on a Friday and Saturday night to help with childcare costs. This meant that at the weekends I would look after the children while she was sleeping during the day, and then she would take care of them through the week. On those weekends singlet Ian would come over on the Saturday – he loved playing with the children, and after they were fed and put to bed we would spend the evening playing PGA Golf tour or EA Sports Football on the Sega Megadrive. We had Lauren's second birthday party on the 30th August '97, and Ian stayed over that night. In the morning I was in the kitchen making breakfast while Ian and Dana were in the lounge playing golf. I had decided to put the little black and white TV on, which was perched high up on a shelf. To my surprise, the news reader mentioned that Dodi, Princess Diana's boyfriend, had been killed in a car crash. I opened the serving hatch and shouted.

"Oh god, Dodi's dead!" I exclaimed. They carried on playing.

I had returned to the TV when the shocking revelation that Diana had also been killed in the same car crash was announced.

"Diana's dead as well," I shouted through the hatch. They didn't believe me.

"Quick, turn over, seriously, it's true."

The TV went on and we all sat there in shock digesting the news, unable to take it in.

A week later on the 6th of September, Dana, myself, and the children had joined her sister Phillipa and boyfriend Dean travelling to France for a holiday. We crossed the Channel on the ferry and while normally people going on holiday would be excited, the mood on the boat was very sombre as passengers packed around the TV screens to watch Diana's funeral. Going away for a holiday was the perfect distraction from the tragic events that had occurred, which had affected the whole country.

There was a change about to happen in my work situation. I had been made aware that a colleague, who worked the north east area of the country for Swizzels, was going to retire at the end of 1998. Three years prior to this, I had made it known to the company that I would be interested in moving to the north to take over. Dana was from there, all her family lived in the region, and it would make sense to the company that an experienced salesman should take over the area as it was one of their biggest. The initial reaction from my then boss was that it would be ok but I could live no further north than Wetherby where Bernard, the retiring rep, lived. I wasn't happy with this notion. Wetherby is one and a half hours from the north east, we needed to be near to family as it meant we could get help with the children if we needed it, plus be able to socialise regularly. It would be no good us living in Wetherby, 76 miles away! However, bosses change, and nearer the time my boss was a scouser called Alan, who put the wheels in motion and made sure it was going to happen at the end of the year.

THE LOSS OF A FRIEND

I recall one afternoon in May of that year, singlets Ian, Phil and myself had spent the afternoon playing golf at Worldham, and afterwards, as Phil dropped off Ian and myself at my home in Rookswood we invited him to join us at the Double Axe pub for a few drinks, which he declined. That was the last time I ever spoke to Phil.

Our children had caught chicken pox and Dana rang Julie, Phil's wife, to let her know in case her children had any symptoms. Phil answered the phone, said thanks to Dana for letting them know, and then told her that they didn't ever want to see us again, and that we were to have no contact with them at all, ever! When I returned home from work Dana told me what had happened. What the fuck! What has happened? Why don't they want to see us again? I had known Phil from our days together at Gallaher's, 15 years ago. When he moved to Alton we had been inseparable; as I have said previously, he was like a brother to me. We were each other's best men, Dana and I were godparents to their children, we helped them move house, we socialised all the time at each other's houses, we had meals together, and he and I shared girlfriends, we were mates. I was at my wits' end. I couldn't sleep, I kept thinking about it, I just didn't understand. Why? It was like a bereavement, like someone had died. I kept thinking back to the day we played golf and when he dropped us off. What did I do? I recalled a conversation while playing golf where I told him I had been to the house of another Gallaher colleague, and I deliberately started flirting with his wife, in jest, and she responded to me, winding him up. It was just fun. Had this upset Phil? Why would it? What's it got to do with him? Had I done the same to Julie? I know that I always complimented Julie on her cooking skills; she was a great cook. Did this make him jealous as well? Phil's moods had shown themselves before, notably when we all went to the Isle of Wight for the weekend. Julie was pregnant at the time, and Dana and I were pretty new to each other, so as we were sat in the back of the car we kept laughing with each other about our bedroom antics. Phil was driving and I felt that he got pretty mad, speeding through the country lanes recklessly, narrowly avoiding disaster. When I had a quiet moment with him, I told him that if he wanted to kill himself he should make sure not to involve us. Another time Phil asked Dana a medical question about him getting a breast reduction, and I jokingly said that I had always admired his breasts. It was a joke, a joke between friends, two very close friends, it was my humour. Was that the reason? Every conversation I had ever had with Phil got played over and over in my mind – was I over the top? Did I go too far with my joking? I really had to have a good look at myself, whether I should ever make personal jokes again. Was it because we were moving over 300 miles away? Was he annoyed about that? Did that upset him? I spoke to singlet Ian and Andy, and asked them if they knew what the problem was. They both knew nothing, at least Ian didn't, he would have told me if he knew, we were pretty close. Singlet Andy, I wasn't so sure, he might have known but he never disclosed anything. During that year singlet Ian and I had been working weekends for a catering company, not every weekend, but when we were required to attend very posh events, set in marquees in the grounds of posh houses in the country. It was a form of silver service, setting up the tables correctly, place settings and cutlery set to perfection, serving meals, walking around with hors-d'oeuvres and platters, and serving drinks. Phil's wife Julie was also involved on the catering side, so we saw each other at these events. I had the opportunity to ask her what had happened. Would she tell me what we had done? Her reply was the same every time: "ask Phil". "But he doesn't want to speak to me," I said. She would always smile and say the same thing: "You'll have to ask Phil". From Julie's reaction, it only seemed to be an issue with Phil, and not both of them. My inner turmoil went on for months and months. If Phil wanted to punish me for some reason then he had succeeded. To this very day I still do not know, and I never will do, but the pain has subsided over the years, just like after a bereavement you do mend, but you don't forget.

OUR MOVE NORTH

We put our house in Rookswood up for sale in the month of May, in readiness for my new position at Swizzels in the north east, and by chance we actually found the buyers ourselves who were friends of friends. As we were also on the market via an estate agent, we negotiated a reduced fee due to the fact that we had found the clients. Dana and I had also been to Sunderland to look for properties and had found a lovely four bedroomed house in Ashwood Terrace, so contracts were exchanged and completed on 2nd October. We sold Rookswood for £96,000 and bought Ashwood Terrace for £86,000, so we had some spare cash to make improvements. Ashwood Terrace was enormous compared to Rookswood, at least twice the size. There is a small garden with a drive at the front, and through the front door is a massive glass-fronted porch which led into the hallway. Ahead was an extended kitchen, albeit dated by the luminous green design, a serving hatch on the left fed into a dining room which had two narrow doors through to the living room. Upstairs were three large bedrooms and a bathroom, with stairs up to an office area and another bedroom in a converted loft. Out the back was a decent sized garden with a carport and an up and over garage door. The house certainly needed work done to it. We immediately installed double glazing throughout as the windows had been painted shut over the years and presented a danger if there was a fire. Under the carpets in the lounge and dining room were wooden floorboards which I sanded down and varnished. In 2004 we had the kitchen ripped out and redesigned, with a granite covered island and a double oven seven-burner cooker installed. These were the only two requests I had for the new kitchen; the rest was left to Dana to design. At the same time as the kitchen installation, we had a large area opened up between the kitchen and dining room where the old serving hatch was to enable walking access through. A few years later we gutted the bathroom and had a new free-standing bath and separate shower installed along with a toilet and sink. The downstairs toilet also had a shower in it, so we took the shower out and installed a washing machine in its place to make more room in the kitchen.

My work up north for Swizzels began in earnest, and I covered an area from Newcastle in the north to Sheffield in the south, west to Halifax/Bradford/Leeds and east to Grimsby. Primarily I called on cash-and-carry outlets, nationally and independently owned, and wholesale customers who tended to be part of buying groups. These accounts were not open to the public, they served the retail outlets and shops in the area. I had a regular cycle of customers which involved negotiating orders in call, arranging displays and relaying fixtures. Some orders could be as big as two or three thousand boxes; however, as the years went by those national accounts moved more towards central delivery, where Swizzels would deliver to their central warehouse and the stock would be distributed to the depots. This meant that order capture in call stopped, and the thrill of gaining an order went with it. The calls became more representation-based, discussing stock levels, ranges stocked and local activity. We would have sales meetings on a quarterly basis, headed by the sales director David. The Christmas meeting was normally held on a middle Friday in December quite regularly at the Grimstock Hotel at Coleshill, where on occasions I would provide the evening's entertainment in the form of a quiz. I had held a pub quiz before and enjoyed the question planning involved in staging one. It also meant that I was in charge, my decision was final and I got to take centre stage for once where my voice would be heard. When the evening had finished and the sales director went to bed, a senior manager would stay up with us as we sat around having a drink, making sure we didn't drink too much. I was in my 40s and I felt like I was being babysat. God, I think I know how much I can drink and still be sensible at the meeting the next day! That was the problem, the meeting was held on the Friday after the Thursday evening's entertainment, so no-one could really let their hair down. This was eventually addressed some years later when we had a change of sales director, and the meeting was moved to the Thursday. We would all have accommodation in a hotel, and after a lovely meal in a nearby restaurant, we would then have entertainment booked in a bar or similar establishment which would continue until one decided to go to bed. Usually, I'm told the last one standing would regularly be the new sales director Mark! All the expense was generously covered by Swizzels, or more importantly, sanctioned by the younger family generation that was to take over the reigns over the years. At the sales meetings there were some big characters, and in later years when the marketing department were involved at the meetings, there could be as many as 25 people sat around the table. I felt insignificant, so instead of trying to be heard, I would resort to the behaviour I indulged in at school and make a funny joke or quip. I was never afraid of making a fool of myself and at future Christmas meetings when Christmas jumpers were a must, I would always wear a silly looking Christmas hat throughout the whole meeting.

Emily started attending St Mary's Catholic Primary School while Lauren followed her to the same school a year later. St Mary's was a quarter of a mile away from home, and due to their age they were collected by an after-school club called Hopscotch, which they would attend until I could pick them up. The girls' personalities were starting to develop. While Emily didn't stop talking, Lauren was the opposite, and was a shy girl. When they were younger Emily did all the talking for Lauren, but as Lauren got older her confidence grew and now, if we are on a walk, Lauren doesn't stop talking! Dana had always been a talker as well, so it is no surprise that they both follow in their mother's footsteps. As the girls were growing up, I gave them pocket money on a weekly basis. They used to get £2 pocket money every week. I used to have a chart on the wall and every time one of them was naughty I would cross off 5p. I would enter their bedroom and the room was untidy.

"Right, who made that mess?" I would say.

"It was Lauren," said Emily.

"Ok, Lauren, that's 5p I'm crossing off your pocket money," I said.

Next time I go in: "Who broke that?"

"It was Lauren," Emily would say. And I would cross off another 5p from Lauren's allowance.

Again, I enter their room. "Right, who spilt that?"

"It was Lauren," Emily would say.

Come Saturday morning we would go for a walk down town, Emily would be smiling and skipping along with her £2 in her pocket, Lauren would be clutching her 35p! On another Saturday we set off for town, Emily started to tell me about her dream. When we got to town 20 minutes later, she still hadn't finished. Every morning before I went to work I would have a shave, and Lauren would observe this ritual on occasions. One day she emerged from the bathroom with small red cuts all across her chin, having attempted to copy me. Emily was a bed wetter, and regularly had accidents. She had previously been given an inflatable armchair which had been used, deflated, and stored under her bed. One day I decided to clear out her room and I pulled the deflated chair out from under the bed, only for me to be covered in cold wet piss that had seeped through her mattress and settled in the folds of the plastic chair.

Around this time Dana had started studying for her nurse practitioner degree, which would take her three years. To help her I would take the burden of the children away to let her study. Even so, there was a strain put on our marriage, and the arguments were regular. We would have shouting matches in front of the girls, something that I regret. On one occasion in the kitchen, Dana threw a cup at me which missed and went through one of the small, panelled windows on the kitchen door. I was furious because the glass splintered into the hallway, I thank god the girls were not behind it. In a marriage, I've come to believe that both husband and wife think they each do the most around the house, she thinks she does all the work and he thinks he does it all. One thing is for sure: it's a partnership, no-one is going to give you a medal for washing up or filling the dishwasher. I have always been hands-on with the children and with the housework. I was never made to help Mum when I lived at home, whereas Dana and her two sisters worked to a rota set by their mother. I don't need to be told to do something because, to me, it's natural to want to improve your living standards by cleaning and tidying up, whereby Dana hates being told what to do, probably brought about by being ordered around by her mum. When the children were in nappies I got stuck in – I had to when Dana worked nightshifts. One particular incident with Lauren I have never forgotten. She had soiled her nappy with a form of diarrhoea and was wearing a babygrow. Unfortunately, the mess had squeezed up out of her nappy and onto her stomach and back, leaving me with no other option. The scissors came out and I had to cut the garment off of her and then stick her in the bath. Singlet Andy, on the other hand, was proud of the fact that he had only changed a few of his daughters' nappies, a number that he could count on his fingers! I loved getting involved with the girls, having to shower them, and being called to wipe their arses! When they went to bed I would read them a bedtime story and then, I would rub their shoulders while they fell asleep. I often smile to myself when I think that their future husbands will be expected to do the same thing.

Christmas was always a special time. I loved propelling the notion that Santa Claus would be bringing them their presents, the look of wonder on their faces was priceless when they were younger. I loved it! I wanted to give them something that I missed out on when my dad died, I'm sure he would have been the same as me. I kept the secret of Santa going for many years, at least that's what I want to believe. But when I have spoken to the girls now they are older, they make out that they only went along with it to keep me happy, that they knew the secret but they didn't want to spoil my fun! My fun? If I'm honest it was my fun, I loved it more than anything. Maybe they did know the secret; if that's the case, then I'm glad they didn't let on because it made me happy and it shows us that we have brought up two beautiful girls that have a great deal of empathy for others.

My work took me away one night every two weeks when I worked Doncaster and Grimsby on the Tuesday, and then drove over the Humber Bridge to Hull where I would stay in the Kingston Theatre Hotel. It was in this hotel that at 1am on 27th February 2008, while I was asleep, that I was suddenly shaken violently from top to bottom in my bed, the building vigorously swaying back and forth, the ground rising and falling as an earthquake hit the area 15 miles south of Grimsby. It measured 5.2 on the Richter scale, and surprisingly, there was no structural damage despite the feeling that I was on a roller-coaster ride and had witnessed the building swaying about. Apart from meetings when I might stay away the night before, this was the only regular time I spent away from home, and I became a regular in the hotel, and was on first name terms with the proprietors of a very good Indian restaurant nearby. Another two-weekly routine in my portfolio took me to Stockton 31 miles down the road from home, where I would be responsible for the central orders for all Batley cash-and-carry outlets in the country, spending most of the day ordering stock by line by depot for 31 depots. However, when the central buying was reassigned to their depot in Birmingham, it meant I had to spend another night away from home. Now it was one night per week. I quite enjoyed my nights away, the girls were now teenagers so they didn't rely on me so much, and when I was away I could indulge in my favourite food at a local Indian restaurant, along with a few beers, all paid for by the company. The only downside was my expanding waistline!

Colin, my old boss who was a senior manager, had decided to retire but was kept on, covering a couple of days' work a month along the south coast towards Devon. The following year when there was a company re-organisation, I had suggested to my boss Ken that I would be willing to cover the south coast from Portsmouth to Exeter and everything between, taking in Bristol and North Devon. In exchange, I could stay at my mum's house in Alton over the preceding weekend, work locally on the Monday and on the Tuesday leave to go on my travels to complete my working week covering the west country. As a bonus to Swizzels, the company would save on Colin's extra wages. This way I could stay at my mum's house once a month, where previously I would only get the chance to visit twice a year. All it would cost the company was a Sunday lunch on expenses so that I could treat Mum and Bill. I had previously also taken on coverage of the Channel Islands and the Isle of Man, so it would also be easier to get to Jersey from Southampton airport.

Due to Mum and Bill getting older, they had to stop going away on holidays. Mum was now 84 and Bill was 87. Four years earlier he had suffered a stroke, and although he recovered well he had to give up his favourite things like dancing, golf and tending an allotment. Dana and I decided that we would take them away for a holiday in the month of November, so we rented a house in Canterbury for a week, where we could give them a break from being at home. It was on this holiday one evening, that I broke the news that I would be visiting and staying with them once a month. They were delighted that their favourite son would be visiting regularly! To my brothers, I say this with my tongue in my cheek, although I know you will still believe it! Over the coming years I was able to visit them monthly – thank you, Swizzels – and to see my brother and sisters who still lived locally.

Now my work area consisted not only of the northern territory Newcastle, Hull, Leeds, Bradford, and Sheffield, but the coastline 170 miles from Portsmouth to Plymouth and Bristol, the Channel Islands, and the Isle of Man. A year later the areas of Cardiff and Swansea were added to my accounts plus additional accounts such as WH Smith at Swindon. My time away from home had increased dramatically, but at this stage of my life I was happy to take the work on board. In fact, when it was required to visit all Booker cash-and-carry outlets in the area, I spent a total of two weeks away, mostly in hotels. The girls were now nearing 20 years old, and were independent of me – although that had happened many years ago when on one of our weekly walks to town, Emily asked me if I minded not holding her hand! I was devastated but I understood her reasoning: she was growing up, and I had to let them grow and go. Thank goodness Lauren still held my hand, for a little while longer at least.

THE SECRET
TO MARRIAGE

Over the years, Dana and I have grown closer together, and I believe a lot of this is down to laughing. We laughed together the first time we met, and we have not stopped laughing. Yes, we have had tough times, but we have come out the other side stronger. A marriage needs laughter, you should be able to take the mickey out of each other, and both laugh. My comic timing and witticism stemmed from my childhood, as a way of brushing over serious issues, covering up sadness, of trying to be popular, and most of all, wanting to make people laugh. I often wonder if I am sad underneath, but it's not a place I am willing to go to. I know I was only three years old when my dad died, but have I really grieved? Maybe the joking is a way of covering it up. I can shed a tear watching Undercover Boss USA or at a happy moment in a film, the tears will well up in my eyes, but I push them back, not wanting to show my emotions. My voice struggles sometimes, my throat feels blocked and the words don't come out, so in the moment, I stop talking and a tear will roll down my cheek. I want to make people laugh, it makes me happy to see them laugh. Laughter is so important, especially in your relationship. At Christmas time, in Dana's Christmas card, over the past 10 years I have taken to giving her an annual appraisal. I will write three positive things she has done in that year and I also write three negative things that she can improve on for the coming year. When I have mentioned this to my male friends their reaction is 'what the fuck! My wife would kill me'. But no, Dana looks forward to her card every year, because it makes her laugh. I tell Dana she is the most intelligent person I know – Lauren says I don't know many people! But we laugh about it. For us, it's the glue that keeps a marriage together. When Sunday dinner came around, the fun time was around the kitchen sink, when the washing up had to be done. When I had a dish that needed to be scrubbed rather than going in the dishwasher, I would hand it to the girls and say, 'this one's a hand job'! Sexual innuendoes have been commonplace in our house for years, talking about sex and bodily functions has been a regular topic. I have learnt a lot about the menstruation cycle living in a house full of females! Emily and Lauren have grown up with laughter and they are both in relationships where they laugh with their partners. It's a good foundation to have. Lauren in particular has developed an amazing knack for comic timing, whether in conversation or by text; I have taught her well. Emily has a loud raucous laugh which fills the room with joy and pleasure when we are all together as a family.

RETIREMENT

After six years working my expanded territory, I came home from my travels after being away for a week in February, and something hit me. I told Dana, I didn't want to do this anymore. I have had enough staying away for work and I have had enough of working for Swizzels. At that time, I was nearing 28 years' service, and over those years I was rarely off work ill and I always made myself available to take on the next step for the company. Whatever I was asked to do, I did it. However, something was telling me to stop; it wasn't planned, it was a feeling. The day after our March 2019 sales meeting, I was scheduled to spend time with the sales director. Over lunch I announced to Mark that I wanted to retire early, but that I was happy to work with the company towards a resolution, the plan being to leave at the end of February 2020 one year later. I effectively gave them nearly a year's notice. I would never have left them in the lurch, it wasn't in my nature and as the company had been good employers, I wanted to be good back to them. It would enable the company to plan changes to account coverage, to employ new sales persons if necessary and to reorganise the sales structure. Little did anyone know what was about to happen in 2020, just one month after I was to leave. The date for me to leave was set for 28th February 2020, and just one week previous, on Friday 21st, Emily got married to Josh, which was a great celebration in our family. I had spent most of the previous year planning my father-of-the-bride speech, and my aim was to embarrass her as best as possible. But how do I get one on Josh? I looked back through our old videotapes of when the girls were young and I found one of Emily, four years old, dressed in her fairy costume with wings and a wand, prancing around the kitchen singing "It must be a Patrick, it must be a Patrick". So, I played the video to the guests and explained that every father wants to make their daughters' dreams come true, so with documentation in hand, I proceeded to present to Josh the certificate from the National UK Deed Poll office where I had had his name changed from Josh to Patrick, a new driving licence with his photo on, and a new passport also accompanied with a photo, which were met with howls of laughter from the guests! Of course, the documents were fake. We had a wonderful day that day, an intimate wedding with about 35 guests, and we were so lucky to have it just before the world suffered a pandemic. Just three weeks later, after news coming from China about a new disease called Covid-19, the UK went into lockdown, virtually everything stopped, and the country closed down. Looking back, I felt so lucky that I got out before the pandemic, I'm not sure how I would have coped working from home constantly. One day a week was fine, but five days a week and I'm sure I would have gone mad. I was more old school than modern, travelling around and meeting customers was more my style, getting out and about, rather than having Zoom meetings with customers and colleagues. As previously mentioned, it was hard enough physically being in meetings and being heard, let alone as a tiny square on a screen, like I was on University Challenge!

I had been frugal over the years when it came to money – my brothers would say I was 'tight'! However, after Swizzels' final salary pension was closed in 2002, I took to investing money in other forms, and this helped enormously with my savings pot. Along with paying the mortgage off early many years ago, it enabled me to make my retirement decision. At 61 years old I retired, only to be hit by the pandemic in 2020 and through 2021, so I had to make a slow start to my life of leisure. I have never been one to laze around doing nothing, I've always been on the go, making the most of my days. Some people retire and sit around doing nothing; I had plenty to keep me occupied. At 50 years old I managed, after being on the waiting list for five years, to get an allotment on Tunstall Hill, a 112m tropical barrier reef formed 240 million years ago, which overlooks the city of Sunderland. When I worked and it rained at the weekend my plans for the allotment were ruined. Now I am retired, I can visit any day I please; it's nice to have that flexibility in my life. I also play golf regularly, my two golf-playing partners were already retired. We play on a golf course within view of the A1M motorway and seeing all those vehicles travelling up and down the road while I am playing golf is a joy to behold for me. I sympathise with those drivers toiling towards their destinations, something that I did every day. On a beautiful day when the sun is shining, I feel blessed to be on the golf course. I met one of my playing partners not long after I moved to Sunderland in 1998. Being a Southampton supporter, I would visit a local pub to watch them play on Sky TV, and on these regular visits I noticed another guy who always turned up to see the same matches. After seeing him a few times we spoke and I discovered he was also a Southampton supporter who had been living in Sunderland for over 30 years. We would then arrange to meet each other in the pub regularly to watch a football match, mostly Sunday afternoons. After six months of this, Dana asked me what his name was, to which I replied, "I don't know, I've never asked him". His name was Ray, and it turns out that he had exactly the same question from his wife at the same time. You see, guys don't need to know names when you have football in common.

SUMMARY

Emily and Lauren have settled into their relationships with their partners in their new homes. Emily and Josh bought their home just before they got married and Lauren and Nathan bought their first house mid-2021. Both of them have respectable jobs: Emily is an English teacher at a secondary school – you could have guessed that vocation after all the talking she did as a child – and Lauren is a receptionist in a vets' practice. She also has her own business drawing people's pets, which she is incredibly talented at and in great demand, often booked up months in advance. She has a soft spot for animals; I should have known that from the number of soft toys she had as a child. Both Emily and Lauren have two house rabbits each, occupying a bedroom in each of their houses. Dana has caught the bug as well, first starting off with two house rabbits, which she has now doubled up to four, although to be fair to them, all the rabbits have come from animal rescue centres. Dana has been quietly improving her work position, having spent seven years working in a local surgery in Seaham as a practice nurse and then as a nurse practitioner, before moving to a surgery in Peterlee and then eventually to a surgery closer to home in Sunderland. Unfortunately, Mum passed away one day short of her 94th birthday. She had been suffering from dementia. The ability to have a lasting conversation with her had gone, although she retained memories from many years ago. Likewise, Bill died in 2018 one day after his 92nd birthday. He was a remarkable and tremendously loyal person. He spent over 40 years working at the brewery in Alton, he became one of the first Littlewoods pools collectors and spent 51 years collecting coupons. He spent 40 years carrying the Union Jack Standard on the annual Remembrance Day Parade and spent 36 years married to Mum, for which he should have been awarded another medal!

In the writing of my memoirs, I have read the diary from my travels around Europe and letters that I had been sent from people I had met, previously unread for 32 years. It has brought back many memories of the fantastic people I came upon, and my next project will be to try to track them down, using their last known addresses, from Sweden, America, Germany, France, and England. I don't hold out much hope for success, but I would love to find out where they are now, what they have been doing, and how their lives have turned out; I might then be able to add a further chapter.

I am writing my memoirs for my children Emily and Lauren so that they have complete knowledge of my life, from childhood to retirement, from the good parts to the bad parts, and from the laughter to the sadness. Girls, this is for you.

Oh, in case you are wondering who Nitram Drib is, it is my name spelt backwards, a game we used to play as children.

Printed in Great Britain
by Amazon